the
birth

AND
DEATH

of the
cool

the
birth

AND
DEATH

of the
cool

TED GIOIA

Library of Congress Cataloging-in-Publication Data

Gioia, Ted.
  The birth (and death) of the cool / Ted Gioia.
    p. cm.
  Includes bibliographical references and index.
  ISBN 978-1-933108-31-5 (hardcover) / 978-1-68275-015-5 (paperback)
  1. Lifestyles--United States--History--20th century. 2. Jazz musicians--United States. 3. Popular culture--United States--History--20th century. 4. Jazz. I. Title.
  HQ2044.U6G56 2009
  306.0973'0904--dc22

                                        2009018827

Printed in the United States of America

0 9 8 7 6 5 4 3 2 1

Design by Larisa Hohenboken

Fulcrum Publishing
4690 Table Mountain Drive, Suite 100
Golden, Colorado 80403
www.fulcrum.bookstore.ipgbook.com

This work is dedicated in appreciation and gratitude to my teachers and mentors, especially John Ashley, Donald Davie, Martin Evans, Ray Garza, Stan Getz, William Goodfellow, John Heine, Michael Inwood, David Kennedy, Konnie Krislock, Sheldon Meyer, James T. S. Porterfield, Robert Zider, and the Sisters of Providence at St. Joseph School in Hawthorne, California.

Contents

Preface

I now can look back on *The Birth (and Death) of the Cool* with the perspective of almost a full decade. And what do I think today?

Well, to be honest, I wish I could repudiate this book.

Not because it's wrong, but because it's proven all too true.

When I first announced the death of the cool and the rise of a new culture of anger and confrontation, many were skeptical. After all, Barack Obama had just swept into office with promises of a new era of reconciliation, the economy was beginning its recovery from the mortgage meltdown, people were going back to work, and a spirit of optimism was pervasive.

Yet even back then, the deeper fault lines could be felt by those sensitive to the shifting tides of public discourse. Fast forward to the present day, and you now see bad attitudes everywhere. The spirit of coolness and conciliation, laid-back lifestyles and low-key demeanors, has almost completely disappeared from the public sphere. Instead, we are angry and seemingly getting angrier with each passing year. In an increasing number of instances, that anger boils over into brutality and violence, sometimes on a mass scale with casualties in the dozens or hundreds. We can feel the tension everywhere now: on social media, in the news, even (if we are especially unlucky) in our day-to-day lives.

Can anyone continue to deny the end of cool? When I wrote this book, the term *hipster* had clearly lost much of its allure. But nowadays the word has turned into an actual insult, a bitter term of derision—often applied to snobbish and wealthy professionals who, back in the 1950s, would have been snubbed as the antithesis of hip. (Always pay attention when words take on the opposite of their original meaning.) Or consider the shifts in entertainment. When I wrote this book, I could see that comedy routines were changing in response to the death of cool, but even I couldn't anticipate how extreme the shift would be. Just the other day I read about a college campus shutting down a play about 1950s jazz-influenced comedian Lenny Bruce—an eerie return to the censorship that cool era humorists thought they had overcome sixty years ago. We are even going back to burning books, and my only hope now is that we don't return to burning the people who write them.

Honestly, I never wanted to publish a book about the death of cool. I originally planned to celebrate coolness. The world forced me to change the subject of my book. I'm not sure I can forgive it. Even so, there is still much of that initial upbeat vision evident in the pages ahead. I believe, with all my heart and soul, that the culture of coolness was a blessing, a beautiful interlude, and I'm sure that a large dose of that positivity still comes across in the book, despite the epitaph for coolness in the title and text.

And, frankly, I am confident that cool will return.

That's the good news here. I'm convinced that cultural history alternates between periods of cool and hot. Each phase lasts about thirty to forty years, before exhausting itself and giving way to the opposite pole of the dialectic. After the ultra-hot world wars, we had earned the long spell of coolness that makes for the focal point of this work. I suspect you could trace the same shift in American history after the Civil War, but I will leave it to other historians to describe that transition. But for the future, I will stake a prediction: If this book survives until its twenty-fifth anniversary—or, even better, if I survive to write about it—we will be on the brink of a new era, less outraged and more cooperative than our current beleaguered state. We will fight less and tolerate more. We will aspire, once again, to coolness. And the whole culture, with its music and stories and images, will be the first place where this shift will emerge. Songs, in particular, have always served as early indicators of cultural change, and I'm sure that will happen again when we experience the "rebirth" of the cool.

So let me encourage you to read this book in that spirit. When you encounter the glory days of cool in the chapters ahead, remind yourself that they will come again, albeit in a different guise.

And, then, let's all try to be part of making that happen.

TED GIOIA
November 2018

Introduction

For many years, I have been planning to write a history of cool as a cultural concept. I have long been fascinated with this subject, which seems to encompass so many facets of our day-to-day lives. Our sense of the cool impacts the music we hear, the clothes we wear, the places we go, the gadgets we buy, even the people we admire and emulate. I was determined to unlock the mystery of this intangible yet powerful force that pervades virtually every nook and corner of our psyches.

But as I dug deeper and deeper into my research, I was surprised by what I discovered. Cool, I determined, was not a timeless concept, but was a construct of very recent origin. Cool in its contemporary meaning is only a few decades old. But even more surprising, my investigations convinced me that cool was on the decline. This modern form of hipness and trendiness started to fall out of favor during the 1990s, and the process has been accelerating in the new millennium.

The more I probed into this matter, the more fascinating the story became, and the more overwhelming the evidence for a cultural paradigm shift. I could only conclude that I was witnessing what I came to call the death of the cool. Once I knew what to look for, the signs of this transformation were evident everywhere. It could be seen in the media, in prevailing trends and fashions, in business and the broader economy, in popular entertainments and diversions, in politics and social institutions, and, above all, in pronounced attitudinal shifts and changing behavior patterns.

I must admit that I have come to view this change with mixed feelings. I was originally attracted to the subject of the cool because of its charm and swagger, its ability to transform, Midas-like, everything it touched into something golden. In this matter, I was no different from others of my generation who were beguiled by coolness; I, too, wanted to capture a bit of it for myself. Yet, as I studied the psychological underpinnings of my subject, I came to understand that certain inherent flaws within the cool worldview were the cause of its inevitable decline. Coolness had served its purpose and been taken about as far as it could go. For almost two generations, it had served as a touchstone and point of navigation for millions of people, but was now on the verge of exhaustion. Inevitably, it would be replaced by newer, more robust approaches.

My book about the cool thus morphed into a much different book than I had originally planned. Instead of unraveling the mystery of an eternal concept, I am now presenting the story of the birth and death of the cool. I anticipate that readers may find the thesis outlined here controversial, at least as they read the opening pages of my book. But I suspect that the more deeply they get into the story, the more convinced they will become that a fundamental change is under way. Even so, I anticipate that many readers, even after they understand the nature of this transformation, will (like me) have ambivalent and contradictory feelings about the implications of this shift.

I would like to thank the Getty Research Institute in Los Angeles, whose invitation to talk about cool jazz at a conference provided the key catalyst in my reexamination of the cool as a cultural phenomenon. Around that same time, I had been working on an essay on the *Birth of the Cool* recordings by Miles Davis for a book edited by Greil Marcus, and it was the conjunction of these two projects that set in motion the new lines of inquiry that resulted in this book. I also want to express my gratitude to Alan Kurtz, whose feedback on the first draft of this work proved to be invaluable. I must also thank Jesse Sheidlower, Brettne Bloom, Steven Cristol, Vince Mitchell, George Schuller, Bill Guns, Brendan Wolfe, Phil Schaap, and Jeff Sultanof for their help and advice at various stages of this project. However, none of these parties bear any responsibility for the limitations or excesses of the finished work. I also want to acknowledge the contributions of Carolyn Sobczak and her colleagues at Speck Press and Fulcrum Publishing. Finally, I want to thank my wife, Tara, and our sons, Michael and Thomas, for their constant support, without which this book would not be possible.

Can Cool Ever Be Uncool?

It's hard for many to imagine that "cool" could ever go out of style. After all, cool *is* style. Isn't it? And it must be even harder to envision great masses of people not only modifying their concepts, but altering their behavior patterns, embracing ways of living that no longer aspire to coolness. That would be…well, so *uncool*.

But the premise of this book is precisely that. The cool is not a timeless concept. Cool as we know it today only appeared on the scene a short while ago. Its greatest period of cultural impact lasted but a few decades. The concept is now on the wane, and other more vigorous and robust ideas are on the rise that will marginalize and, increasingly, replace it.

The term has become so overused these days that *cool* is now a verbal tic expressing approval of any sort. "You want to go get dinner? Okay, cool!" In this vague manner, *cool* is now applied to anything that is current or popular or even just acceptable. I am not talking about that usage of the term in this book. This loose way of speaking will probably continue long after the essence of the cool as a cultural style has lost its luster—although even casual language will likely adapt to the new state of affairs in time. Rather, I am interested in the larger cultural shift and worldview that overshadow this way of employing the term and made it possible in the first place. The word *cool* did not have this positive meaning a hundred years ago, and the reason it does today is the result of a strange flip-flop in the modern mind that took place around the time Miles Davis released his *Birth of the Cool* recordings, as they later came to be called, around the midpoint of the twentieth century. This change not only influenced how we talk about our lives but—even more potently—altered how we live them. It was more than just a new style (as a fashion designer might use the term), although an obsession with style was one of its defining qualities. Cool went deeper, shaping psyches and characters, and impacting how people dealt with situations and looked at themselves. It is this set of beliefs, values, and behavior patterns, what I call "the cool," that is now under attack and revision.

The cool's first stirrings came from the world of jazz, but soon its influence could be seen in movies, literature, and other cultural spheres. In time, cool even spread into the fabric of everyday American life. It gained momentum as a populist movement, offering a dose of glamour and distinction to all who believed in its promises—promises all the more alluring for the cool vanguard's disregard of class and racial categories, its reveling in precisely those groups who had been excluded from traditional power structures. What started as a lifestyle limited to a few jazz "out-cats"—Bix Beiderbecke, Lester Young, Miles Davis—became a mass movement by the time we got to the 1970s and 1980s. But this paradigm shift was a strange one, moving from the marginalized reaches of society and only gradually seeping into the centers of power and prerogative.

Everybody could play *this* game. That was part of its attraction. Cool offered a fresh, new tone, more ironic and able to shift quickly from above-it-all aloofness to an almost extreme emotional sensitivity. It took delight in image and artifice and transformed everything it touched: fashions, accessories, cars, hairstyles, music, language, mannerisms. It helped if you had money—doesn't it always?—but the new mood also rejected mindless materialism, at least at first (that would change over time, and this shift would itself contribute to cool's looming demise). Back in the day, you could be as cool as the other side of the pillow without a dime in your pocket… provided you had the right attitude. What a glorious concept! Even those who first resisted its influence—corporations, politicians, churches, and various old-school institutions—eventually came on board and (surprise!) often played the game better than the musicians and artists and bohemians who had first established cool's dominance.

In fact, the corporations got *too* good at manipulating the cool…and as a result have accelerated its inevitable decline. But other factors—demographic, psychographic, generational, economic—are also now contributing to the death of the cool. Sociopolitical events (9/11, war, financial meltdowns, and so forth) have no doubt influenced the process, but did not cause it; this is a revolution that has taken place, for the most part, unheralded in big-font headlines. But the results of this shift, little understood at present, will be far-reaching. Forms of entertainment and works of art have long aspired to a cool tone, but they will now find greater inspiration elsewhere, often in the most surprising places. Marketing careers have been built on measuring and manipulating edented media attention to nerds, geeks, and dweebs. The year 2006 witnessed the debut of the anticool TV show *Ugly Betty*, starring America Ferrera as its very unglamorous protagonist. On September 24, 2007, *Chuck* premiered on NBC, a show about a socially inept computer whiz. And on the same day, CBS launched *The Big Bang Theory*, based on the exploits of clueless physicists who have about as much suavity as a secondhand particle accelerator. The show *Beauty and the Geek* has been a success in both the United States and the United Kingdom. Meanwhile, numerous books celebrating nerdiness have shown up on the shelves of your local bookstore: *Geek Chic*, *American Nerd*, *A Girl's Guide to Dating a Geek*, *The Geek Handbook*, and *Nerds: Who They Are and Why We Need More of Them*, to cite just a few examples of this growing subgenre. At this pace, Bill Gates may soon be nudging the hunks and starlets off the covers of the supermarket tabloids.

Then again, you don't need to read a book or magazine or even own a TV to understand the cultural shift now under way. Just listen to the music. Shifts in musical tastes are often the single best indicator of large-scale changes in the air—sometimes revealing new attitudes long before they are picked up by pundits and the print media. Listen to Bob Dylan in a live recording from the Gaslight in 1962 singing "A Hard Rain's A-Gonna Fall," and you can hear the student unrest and protests coming, even though the Gulf of Tonkin Resolution is still two years away. If you were watching Elvis Presley in 1955 and saw what Colonel Tom Parker saw, or were checking out Benny Goodman in 1935, before his rise to the top, you had a glimpse not just of artistic talent in formation, but of the future of the nation. Little wonder that F. Scott Fitzgerald, when trying to sum up his generation, simply called it the Jazz Age, just as the thirties became the Swing Era and the sixties the Age of Woodstock. Ever since the rise of recorded music, songs have pointed the way, defining each generation in ways that no market research can match. Just as economists have their index of leading economic indicators, students of social change need to examine these leading indicators blaring away on the radio 24/7.

In later chapters, we will trace how the concept of cool was first shaped by musicians and only later picked up by the general public. But what do more recent musical trends tell us? Here we see the death of cool writ large and reaching almost crisis proportions for the industry. The record labels have grown more and more focused on packaging and promoting the coolness of musicians on their rosters, but with less and less impact on the marketplace. Not too long ago, many leading acts could sell a million copies of a CD during its first week after launch, but nowadays this hardly ever happens. And even when a new act has a hit, the industry has come to expect the inevitable sophomore curse, with the follow-up release falling far short of the debut. In the new millennium, music careers enter a tailspin almost before they have begun.

Why? The industry blames downloading and file sharing and technology shifts. Yet a number of surprising success stories in the music industry reveal that people have a tremendous hunger for less-packaged musical fare, for songs that cut through the commoditization of cool and hark back to a more authentic sound and style. The music moguls were stupefied when Norah Jones's 2002 CD, *Come Away with Me*, built on simple, heartfelt singing backed by a small combo, sold twenty million copies. This vocalist has emerged as one of the most successful recording artists of modern times—and has done it by performing songs that sound as though they might have been composed before World War II (and in some instances, they actually were). Yet the industry had experienced an even more dramatic warning signal a few years earlier, when the soundtrack to *O Brother, Where Art Thou?* climbed to the top of the charts, earning a gold record—and then went platinum, and double platinum, and eventually achieved eight-time platinum status. This CD opened with a work song sung by prisoners at a Mississippi penitentiary—a performance never even intended to be a commercial recording!—and then followed up with old-timey songs in a bluegrass, blues, or folk vein. If you were throwing an anticool party, this CD would be your first choice for background music.

Recent years have witnessed an increasing number of these anomalies—hit records from sources that seem to be completely out of touch with the cool trappings of commercial music. In 1994, the Benedictine Monks of Santo Domingo de Silos went triple platinum by recording eleventh-century music and reached the number three spot on the *Billboard* pop charts. Buena Vista Social Club, featuring the music of virtually unknown Cuban musicians who had hardly been well-known at their peak during the 1940s and 1950s, sold eight million copies of their 1997 CD—far more than any recording of Cuban music in history—and earned a place as one of only two releases not recorded in English-speaking countries to rank on *Rolling Stone*'s list of the five hundred best albums of all time. In the new millennium, singer Eva Cassidy—who died of melanoma in 1996 at age thirty-three, virtually unknown in the music world— became a posthumous star, selling eight million CDs and almost defining the postcool tone with her rejection of hip poses and ironic moods in favor of a heartfelt probing into the inner life of her songs. Each of these megahits came as a total surprise to music industry execs who were focused on finding and cultivating acts with more glamour and attitude.

We see the same forces at work in the extraordinary long-term market share gains made by country music recordings—sales of which have doubled during the last two decades and now outsell rap, pop, or R & B styles of music at a time when demographics would seem to favor trendier multiethnic, urban styles. Four out of the top ten best-selling artists in 2007 were country acts, and this style of music is now the dominant radio genre, with more than two thousand stations offering the down-home sound to an apparently insatiable audience. I could cite other examples, from New Age or gospel artists—and we will explore in more detail what the music is telling us later—but the overall picture is all too clear. In less than a generation, we went from *Flashdance* to *Riverdance*, and no one seems to be looking back. The mainstream entertainment industry has become too cool for school, and the public is looking for something with less of a pose, something more down-to-earth.

You can try to measure this shift away from the old-school cool by tracking demographics or looking at the *Billboard* charts, but the biggest change is psychological. The chatty, ironic attitudes that grew up with the birth of the cool—and we will see how irony and cool walk hand in hand—are now on the wane. The death of irony can be seen everywhere, in music, movies, comedy, everyday language. Instead, we see sincerity, directness, and a zero degree of attitude setting the new tone. Just look at *American Idol*, where the cool candidates always lose out to homegrown fare. If a new John Lennon, a new Jagger or Dylan ever arrives on the scene, you won't learn about it on this show. Instead, we see overweight Ruben Studdard beating pretty boy Clay Aiken; simple country sweetheart Carrie Underwood trouncing hip Bo Bice; gray-haired Taylor Hicks from Birmingham, Alabama, getting the nod over sultry Katherine McPhee, the glamour girl from L.A. Even tried-and-true rockers, such as bartender-turned-singer David Cook, need to adopt a humble and lovable attitude in order to win this star-making competition. There is some heavy irony here, since the producers of this hit show try to package and present it as the epitome of cool—a goal repeatedly subverted by the fans who pick the winners and losers.

The same phenomenon is evident on other competition "reality" shows. The winner of the debut season of *Nashville Star*, the country music equivalent of *American Idol*, was overweight and unattractive Buddy Jewell, who defeated drop-dead gorgeous Miranda Lambert, largely because of the heart and raw authenticity of his singing. Kurt Nilsen took top honors at the *World Idol* competition in Europe, despite looking like (in the words of one of my acquaintances) "the mutant child of Louie Anderson and Alfred E. Neuman." The more recent rise to fame of Susan Boyle on *Britain's Got Talent* and her rapid conquest of the US market presents an equally striking example of this phenomenon at work. The lack of glamour and hipness somehow enhances the appeal of these against-the-grain stars. Their victories in fan-driven competitions run completely counter to the conventional wisdom of the entertainment industry, which for decades has built its talent base almost exclusively by signing and promoting performers who have the highest coolness quotient. This pervasive, but little recognized, shift in the modern mind-set is one of our best indicators that something new is in the air.

Or look at the world of humor. Comedians now talk about the new "naturalist strain" in jokes—and the back-to-basics trend they describe is very similar to what we are seeing in other cultural spheres, from music to media, politics to the pulpit. "If you watch old movies or shows that go back the last couple of decades," comments Conan O'Brien, "it was mostly wisecracks. People wanted certain comedic premises in everything. Now people are wary of comedy that seems too prepackaged. People like this new naturalism, if that's the right word to use." Jenna Fischer, of *The Office*, remarks, "That's sort of the new horizon for comedy now—finding the places that aren't the punch line." Lorne Michaels, the creator of *Saturday Night Live*, concurs: "There's fashion in everything—particularly in comedy." [5] *Saturday Night Live* continues to thrive, but only by stepping back from the big punch lines and slick shtick of the past.

It came as no surprise to see the same shift so prominently displayed in the 2008 presidential campaign. Remember when Bill Clinton put on sunglasses and played the saxophone on Arsenio Hall's show, captivating the electorate with his cool attitude? Remember him answering questions about the relative merits of boxers and briefs? Those days are gone. Barack Obama stands out as a textbook example of the new earnestness, the irony-free politician. His seriousness, his almost total rejection of glitziness and attitude—all the more striking given the historical connections, which we'll explore in later chapters, between the cool and African American culture—tap directly into the new Zeitgeist. Yet it is all too revealing that during the campaign, John McCain tried to make his opponent seem as cool as possible, even evoking comparisons to Britney Spears and Paris Hilton in his attack ads—charges all the stranger given Obama's almost complete indifference to the cool trappings of celebrityhood. Many observers were puzzled: since when was coolness a crime? McCain, for his part, tried to embrace the unpretentious and natural in his campaign, never more markedly than in his choice of the moose-hunting mayor of Wasilla, Alaska, as his running mate. When had two candidates worked so hard to be unhip? But in this contest, Barack Obama had a decided advantage: he virtually embodies the new postcool tone. When Obama was asked about his views on boxers or briefs—the question that Bill Clinton had answered so glibly on MTV in 1992—he responded without hesitation: I don't answer *those* questions. Yes, times have changed.

This contrast in styles is tending to confuse the media pundits, who are still caught up in the old paradigm. Writing in *The New Republic*, Michelle Cottle struggles to come to grips with Obama's anticool demeanor: "If one were to gather together a dozen of our society's key arbiters of cool—ad execs, movie stars, fashion designers, music critics, pollsters, suburban tweens—and instruct them to generate the profile of a 'cool' politician, what are the odds that their efforts would result in a gangly, jug-eared, overeducated, workaholic with a fondness for Scrabble?" She continues her rant, critiquing Obama's reading habits, his choice of TV shows, even his dancing moves ("If what we've witnessed thus far of his dancing is any indication, he is somewhat rhythmically challenged"), and concludes, "Not to denigrate our freshly minted president, but, when you tick through some of the basics, Barack Obama comes across as an inveterate dork."[6] Yet what Cottle and others miss is that this very refusal to act the part of the hipster adds to Obama's appeal and enhances his status, defining a new chapter not only in American politics but also in the broader culture, where the postcool tone is now in the ascendancy.

These forces—whether attitudinal or aesthetic, spiritual or practical, political or quotidian—are implicitly a renunciation of the cool. Coolness, from this emerging perspective, is viewed with suspicion. It is, at best, a sign of shallowness, a living on the surface level of appearances. At worst, it is a marketing ploy, a way of manipulating individuals and groups in the name of the almighty dollar. And though there are still large forces trying to sustain the coolocracy, they are mostly corporations whose very clumsiness and heavy-handedness in pursuing their interests will only accelerate their decline.

There is a recurring commercial that I have seen more than a hundred times by now, advertising a satellite Internet provider. It features a perky actress hyping the service with a hard-sell routine and the smarmiest smile. At the very close of her spiel, she stares into the camera and asks, "How cool is that?" The obvious answer, which I am tempted to say back to the TV screen, is: "Sorry, my friend, not very cool at all." Even my two children (ages thirteen and eight) laugh at this phony line every time they see this commercial—they may not know much of the world, but they have seen about a *million* ads during their short time on this planet and can tell corporate hype when they see it. Face the facts, this is where cool usually thrives today, in the realm of the bogus and exaggerated—where we are *told* what is cool right before we get told what it costs. The fact that the youngsters are the quickest to mock these examples of faux cool tells you that a hard rain is gonna fall soon on some clueless corporate marketers.

The backlash is already in full swing. I have noticed in e-mails (mostly from high-tech folks younger than me) that some have taken to deliberately misspelling the word. "I know that it isn't kewl." "Yes, that is so kewl." They take delight in making fun of this word, which seems to stand for so much that they despise. There is even a new search engine, a competitor to Google, called Cuil (www.cuil.com), which has latched on to the joke not just to exempt itself from the cool, but to establish its credibility by explicitly ridiculing the very concept. The revenge of the nerds? Perhaps. Maybe these are just a bunch of cynics. And as I mentioned before, the casual use of cool as a vague term of affirmation may well linger on indefinitely. But this peculiar sense of embarrassment that increasingly seems to accompany the word is telling us that, in some circles at least, cool has stopped being kewl.

In short, a conflict in worldviews is under way right now. On the one hand, a host of institutions and people—in business, media, entertainment, fashion, and other fields—are struggling to keep the old rules intact. These folks want, even more, they *need*, to maintain the outward focus and facile trend-following so characteristic of the Age of Cool. On the other hand, more and more people—the audience and consumers, so to speak, for these efforts—are increasingly resisting. The postcool mandate is to look for something more real, more authentic, less manipulated by these arbiters of taste. These two forces meet head-on every day now, and the results are sometimes strange and puzzling.

Here is the reason for the glut of "reality shows" that aren't very real at all, but reveal traditional media scrambling to adjust to the new state of affairs. Here is the reason why more and more people are skipping the latest TV show or summer blockbuster in order to surf YouTube and MySpace and Facebook, where they can experience the creativity of real people in real-life situations. Here is the impetus for more people getting their news from blogs than from the talking head du jour on CBS or NBC. When it comes to the postcool, homespun amateur efforts have a decided advantage over slick professional fare. Yes, the postcool is also susceptible to corporate manipulation, but it is a more challenging task, and (as we shall see) often susceptible to angry backlash from the public.

Even serious literature is shifting in response to the new world-view. "Sincerity is in," writes Scott Turow in *The New York Times Book Review* as he surveys the current state of fiction. "Since 9/11, American readers have shown an appetite for simple tales told with becoming directness."[7] Turow doesn't mention it, but the same trend appears to be under way in the world of poetry. Critics have even begun to talk of "a New Sincerity Movement" among contemporary poets. Here too, the impact of 9/11 is seen as setting off the new tone of warmth and directness and its associated rejection of pointed irony, but many other factors contribute to its emergence, as we shall see as we probe this surprising Zeitgeist. "My position is irony is dead," Jesse Thorn has stated in explanation of this shift in temperament. "But at the same time, just to return to old-fashioned sincerity, and particularly the kind of sentimentality that that draws in with it…we don't need it. So that's why we've created the New Sincerity."[8]

A generation ago, leading critics would have seen the future of literature growing out of the cool jazz–inflected prose of Pynchon, the dazzling wordplay of Nabokov, the multilayered meanings of Joyce, the complexity of Pound and Eliot. Instead, we have the literary equivalent of reality TV. Turow seems more than a little surprised by the dominance of "straightforward tales about good people trying to lead good lives, who believe in love and friendship, work and honor and charity, the prosaic but immense forces that dignify most of our lives." With popular authors, from Mitch Albom to Khaled Hosseini, the new tone is straight from the heart, without flash or attitude. Even if one looks at the influential highbrow fiction writers of recent years, one is struck by how little experimentalism is in their works, by how much of their writing is focused on the raw and unadorned human dimensions of their narratives, rather than on literary razzle-dazzle. In contrast, attempts to capture the cool mood of the moment, such as Tom Wolfe's 2004 novel, *I Am Charlotte Simmons*, or Jonathan Lethem's *You Don't Love Me Yet* from 2007, increasingly get a tepid response or are actually derided (as when Wolfe's book earned a Bad Sex in Fiction award from London's *Literary Review*). In fiction, as with *Talk* and *Real Simple*, trendy loses out to homespun.

Who can doubt that the corporate coolhunters are in disarray in the face of all this uncoolness? Cable TV networks run round-the-clock coverage of Britney, Paris, and other manufactured icons of cool—and then wonder why a sense of exhaustion sets in and viewers lose interest. The media outlets that thrive on paparazzi incidents and juicy gossip now feel obliged periodically to denounce these same tawdry spectacles—they can't seem to live with them or without them. Music industry execs launch new acts that are selected not for their musicianship (heaven forbid!) but for their coolness—and then wonder why CD sales are plummeting year after year. TV networks churn through concepts looking for the next cool sitcom, but the half-lives of these shows continue to decline, and only a few brave insiders admit that they may be facing an irreversible decline, driven by the phoniness of the genre—the audience wants something more real, less contrived, not half so hip. The old approaches haven't disappeared, but they don't get the same results anymore. A feeling of saturation permeates the scene.

The responses to these crises reveal both the real, underlying reasons for them as well as the desperation of those who benefit from the old paradigm. In their attempts to stanch the bleeding, the ruling powers try to mimic the new tone. In 2007, musician Marié Digby launched a successful grassroots campaign to promote her music on YouTube and MySpace, and her videos were viewed more than fifteen million times by site visitors. Her popular "Unfold" video depicted her sitting with a cheap-looking guitar in what looks like a downscale apartment—you can see the bathtub with various toiletries scattered around it in the background—singing of unrequited love. But two weeks after this video showed up on YouTube, *The Wall Street Journal* blew her cover. Digby never told her fans that she was under contract to Walt Disney's Hollywood Records label. In fact, in a box on her MySpace page where she needed to note "Type of Label," she posted "None." Only after *The Wall Street Journal* started making inquiries did Digby change it to "Major."[9]

When Digby appeared on Carson Daly's late-night talk show, the host told his viewers, "I don't think we need a television show to find talent in America, we have the Internet." And Digby played along, gushing, "I just did this YouTube video two months ago and never, ever imagined that it would actually get me on TV or radio or anything like that." In point of fact, Digby got on TV with the help of Hollywood Records' public relations department, which booked her on the show. What a strange change of affairs from past decades, when an artist signed to a major label would shout it to the hills, proud of this break that promised instant stardom. But

Marié Digby realized that nowadays, instead of being a cool star with connections, it is far better to be an ordinary girl, as much like everyone else as possible.

When Digby's CD, *Unfold*, was finally released in April 2008, the Hollywood/Disney crew pulled out all the stops to resuscitate the hipness of an artist who was already cooling off before her official debut. More behind-the-scenes promotion secured Digby a spot as one of five artists featured in Gap's spring 2008 Sound of Color ad campaign. An aggressive price promotion enabled Amazon to sell the CD at $5.99, but after a few days hovering outside the top fifty sellers, *Unfold* dropped out of the top one hundred. Two weeks after release, it had fallen out of the top three hundred. A career that launched fifteen million video downloads before her first CD was now sinking once it became openly aligned with a major entertainment megacompany.

Digby, of course, is not an isolated example. The lonelygirl15 controversy on YouTube—in which California filmmakers masqueraded as a sixteen-year-old video blogger in order to develop an audience for their work—showed how effective this duplicitous approach could be. At least for a time. Eventually *Los Angeles Times* reporter Richard Rushfield broke the news that the powerful Creative Artists Agency was linked to the lonely girl, who turned out be twenty-year-old New Zealand actress Jessica Rose. This type of deception has, in fact, become so common that it now has a name: astroturfing. Just as Astroturf (the artificial grass used for many indoor sports facilities) is a phony equivalent of real grass, *astroturfing* is a bogus imitation of a grassroots movement.

Whether pitching a record, a movie, or a political movement, the astroturfers try to hide their clout, money, and elite status behind the facade that their efforts are coming from ordinary people just like you and me. The practice has become so widespread that the Federal Trade Commission felt compelled to jump into the fray in December 2006, insisting that companies must disclose their attempts to manipulate word-of-mouth marketing campaigns by using paid ringers to tout their products.[10] Companies that fail to do so could be subject to cease-and-desist orders or substantial fines ranging from a few thousand to millions of dollars.

This new area of government intervention sent ripples of fear through corporate boardrooms. For corporate manipulation to retain its efficacy in an age of postcool, it is often forced to become indirect and deceptive—this is inevitable given the marketing resistance of the new ethos. Yet now these masquerades are increasingly likely to be exposed. Who knew, for example, that a marketing division of Procter & Gamble had assembled a volunteer team of 250,000 teenagers who would shill for the company's products to family, friends, and acquaintances? Who knew that Sony Ericsson had hired sixty actors to pose as tourists, paying them to walk up to complete strangers in New York and Seattle and ask them to take a photo with the T68i mobile phone and digital camera? Who knew that the good-looking guy or gal ordering a mixed drink from the bartender at a fashionable watering hole was bankrolled by the liquor company? Who knew that the fan in the chat room extolling the virtues of a video game or a motion picture was getting a check from the manufacturer?

The problem with such stealth tactics, however, is that they inevitably backfire. You can fake many things, but reality is not one of them. Remember *The Blair Witch Project*? This successful 1999 indie film emulated a nonfiction documentary pieced together from amateur footage and grossed $248 million—although it only cost a few thousand dollars to make. But the take for *Blair Witch 2* dropped by a stunning $200 million, while the production costs skyrocketed to $15 million. There was no *Blair Witch 3*.

I am reminded of the words of the French writer and diplomat Jean Giraudoux, who once advised: "The secret of success is sincerity. Once you can fake that you've got it made." The arbiters of cool think that following this dicey formula will help them survive and thrive in the midst of the new Zeitgeist. But the general public will be increasingly scornful of hype and spin of all sorts, and they will be especially angry when the corporate spin masquerades as a postcool grassroots movement. The new generation will be truth seekers instead of cool seekers. And technological tools are making hype detection easier and easier all the time. In 2008, liberal-minded John Atcheson and conservatively inclined Todd Herman joined forces in launching SpinSpotter, software that dissects and highlights the bias in news articles. A few months earlier, Virgil Griffith launched WikiScanner—a Web-based tool that allows people to identify businesses and organizations that are making anonymous changes to their own Wikipedia entries. A host of other websites—Labelwatch, Greenwashing Index, OutOfPocket.com, and Doctor Oogle, among others—are contributing to this trend toward transparency and straight talk. And this is merely the start.

The beginning of the end for cool was signaled when it became commoditized—a process that we will trace in detail in later chapters. Philosophers have a term for this transformation: they call it *reification*. Reification occurs when a relationship between people is treated as though it were an object or commodity. Some social critics use this concept as a tool in decoding economics or class structure. But no contemporary phenomenon is more reified than the cool. What originally was an attribute of individuals, almost a type of charisma or personal magnetism, has been ruthlessly exploited by profiteers and forced to pretend that it exists inside a pair of running shoes, a fragrance, a new style of jeans, a movie, a logo.

But reification is an illusion, a distortion. Its power evaporates as soon as its deception is uncovered. And, experience shows, no one gets fooled forever. The public just becomes more resistant to the attempts to manipulate and influence. Two-thirds of adults now believe that "most businesses will take advantage of the public if they feel they are not likely to be found out," according to a 2004 Yankelovich Partners survey. And one-third of the respondents would accept a lower standard of living in order to live without advertising and marketing. Author Lynn Upshaw muses, "When was the last time you ever heard people *even claim* they would be willing to lower their standard of living?"[11] Consultants David Lewis and Darren Bridger found the same reaction against marketing messages in their research into consumer behavior and have even summed it up in a succinct formula: the developed world first moved from "scarcity to abundance," and the next move is from "abundance to authenticity."[12]

Here is our current landscape in a nutshell: ordinary and everyday are increasingly knocking the socks off cool and hip. But the bosses and pundits are often the last to know. When the cats with cool attitude are voted off of *American Idol* while the down-home gals and guys, many of them so unstylish that it is almost laughable, come back week after week, the "experts" cry conspiracy. There *must* be a group of ironic, cool people who are *deliberately* picking the worst contestants. Yet this tells you more about the old establishment—run by ironic people who might do just that—than about contemporary America. The new generation will not waste their vote to express an ironic and sarcastic state of mind; they don't have half of the irony of their parents' generation. In short, we have come a long way from the 1960s. The truest thing you could say about the people who will be running things in a few years is also the simplest: what you see is what you get.

But if cool has finally become uncool, what can you possibly do for an encore? Our first step in answering this question must be to look at how we reached this peculiar and unprecedented situation.

The Mystery of My Parents' Lifestyle

I can't recall my parents ever calling anything cool—except maybe the weather. Mom and Dad were *not* hip people, and I could make a long list of the words and phrases I never heard them use. Dad was unaware that adjectives like *groovy* or *rad* or *tubular* existed. I never once heard him say "Far out, dude" or "This is strictly dullsville, man." Mom never once turned to him and asked: "What's cookin', Daddio?" She never even let out a single "hunky dory" or "peachy keen."

I know what you're thinking. Given my upbringing, it *is* amazing I turned out as cool as I am today!

But there is another word that my parents never used that I want to focus on at this juncture. Here it is: *lifestyle.*

My parents were worriers. They had grown up in the Great Depression and never took anything for granted. They worried every day about bills and necessities, about raising their four children. About how to pay for college tuition when they didn't have the college degrees themselves that might have helped them put aside the required cash. They worried about how they would ever afford to retire. They worried about health care and their extended family, about God and country, and about the state of the world in general.

But they never worried about their lifestyle. Never spoke about it. Never thought about it, as far as I could tell. For them, living itself was hard enough. Trying to do it with some style and panache was outside their scope of understanding. If I had forced the issue with them, tried to get them to talk about trendy fashions or how one projected the image of a cool lifestyle, they would have dismissed such matters as shallow. Or (if they had thought of the word) as decadent.

My parents were not unusual in this regard. America was ostly ignorant of lifestyles until the 1960s—but then things changed rapidly. The term *lifestyle* appeared in the *Chicago Tribune* only seven times during the year 1967, but five years later that same newspaper used the word 3,300 times.[1] Today many newspapers even have lifestyle editors. The media not only uses (and overuses) the term *lifestyle*—which has come to encompass almost anything cool or fashionable or personal with a positive spin—but to a great extent they build their coverage of day-to-day events around it.

Of course, the concept of lifestyle led a subterranean existence long before the *Chicago Tribune* and other newspapers paid much attention to it. The term comes to us from Germany, where it was first employed by sociologists and psychologists. As early as 1900, Georg Simmel used the word in his *Philosophie des Geldes*, but this book was not translated into English until the 1960s. Sociologist Max Weber also discussed lifestyles in his work *Economy and Society*, a collection of writings published posthumously in 1922, but this book, too, was long unavailable in English. Most sources give credit to psychologist Alfred Adler for introducing the word *lifestyle* into the English-speaking world in 1929, with the translation of his *Problems of Neurosis*. Yet these various works, with their specialized and arcane approach to the concept of lifestyle, did little to introduce this strange new word into the vocabulary of the general public.

Nor could they. Even if Adler's *Problems of Neurosis* had jumped to the top of the best-seller list upon its release in English in 1929 (admittedly unlikely, given its candid discussions of polygamy, masochism, perversions, narcotics, and various bizarre fantasies), it could hardly have established lifestyle as a meaningful concept for most Americans. The country was about to enter into an economic free fall: the Great Depression (with its overtones of both financial and psychological malaise), the very upheaval that made my parents so resistant to the concept of lifestyle.

But more to the point, *lifestyle* did not mean the same thing for Adler and Weber as it would to later generations. It had none of the bohemian connotations it would eventually come to possess. In its earliest formulations, the concept of lifestyle was strongly linked to issues of class, character, and culture. The idea that someone could create a fresh new lifestyle from a blank sheet of paper, that the choice of a lifestyle could be a tool in self-actualization and liberation from mind-numbing conformity, a path to a cooler way of being…all this would come much later. And when it arrived, it would change everything in its wake.

The first reference to *lifestyle* in nonspecialized American writing mentioned by the *Oxford English Dictionary* is—interestingly enough—in the context of a discussion of those who "found in the wailing self-pity and crooning of the Negro the substitute for any life-style of their own."[2] The quote comes from Marshall McLuhan, writing in 1947, almost at the same time that the word *cool* was showing up in its modern form in the black community, along with a host of behavior patterns that would later define the cool ethos.

Here we are much closer to the glorious new meaning that the term *lifestyle* would come to occupy for the baby boomer generation, and the connection to African American music in McLuhan's citation cannot be mere coincidence. Over the next two decades, *lifestyle* would morph from a seldom-used bit of academic jargon into the most potent buzzword on the scene. At the close of the sixties, Charles Reich looked back at the decade in his best seller, *The Greening of America*, and enthused: "The meaning of liberation is that the individual is free to build his own philosophy and values, his own life-style, and his own culture from a new beginning."[3] For Reich and the baby boomer generation, lifestyle was not just one more way of describing their individuality—along with height, gender, age, hair color, fingerprints, and so forth. All those other attributes are givens, handed out at birth. Lifestyle was a different metric, one that you could shape yourself with conscious intent and (if you were cool enough) a sense of style and flair.

Reich had found the right message for the times. His paean to lifestyle excited readers from its first appearance in *The New Yorker*, in September 1970. When it was published by Random House, *The Greening of America* shot to the top of the best-seller list. And if anyone had any doubts that a self-actualizing lifestyle was the dominant topic of the day, all they needed to do was look at the other number one best sellers on *The New York Times* nonfiction rankings that year: *Everything You Always Wanted to Know about Sex (But Were Afraid to Ask)* by Dr. David Reuben, *The Sensuous Woman* by "J," *Up the Organization* by Robert Townsend, and other similarly edgy volumes were setting the tone for the era. From the boardroom to the bedroom, people were taking control of their lives and breaking out of the stultifying molds of the past.

Where did these new lifestyle-oriented movements come from? Most commentators at the end of the sixties would have linked them to college students, hippies and longhairs, antiwar protesters and Summer of Love free spirits. But Reich reaches back farther and anticipates our own connection of lifestyle formation with the cool-and-hot jazz postwar counterculture. "Unquestionably the blacks made a substantial contribution to the origins of the new consciousness," he writes. "They were left out of the Corporate State, and thus they had to have a culture and life-style in opposition to the State. Their music, with its guts, contrasted with the insipid white music. Their way of life seemed more earthy, more sensual than that of the whites. They were the first to scorn the establishment and its values."[4] Here was a cosmic shift that had happened, in embryonic form, *before* the sixties, paving the way for the new state of mind, a movement that had more to do with Miles Davis and Muddy Waters than with Harry Truman and Dwight Eisenhower.

It is revealing that Reich—oddly echoing McLuhan—almost instinctively looks to music as his key indicator, akin to the way a stockbroker turns to the Dow Jones Industrials to measure the pulse of the financial world. How strange that this experienced academic, a professor at Yale Law School and former clerk to Supreme Court Justice Hugo Black, would not only cite songs for evidence, but does so from the very first page of his book, where he picks out epigraphs from Woody Guthrie and the rock-pop band The Youngbloods to set the stage for his proclamation of the new moment in history. Reich, in this regard, was spot on. Songs and recordings are often the very first place where these psychographic shifts can be read, long before the newspapers and pundits pick them up. And when the cult of lifestyle began to falter in the late 1990s and new millennium, the music on the airwaves told the tale first, just as it had back in the Age of Aquarius.

Indeed, one of the defining characteristics of the second half of the twentieth century was the growing overlap and blurring between lifestyle categories and aesthetic categories. Starting in the fifties and gaining momentum over the next two decades, average people wanted to lead their lives as though they were works of art, songs or movies or novels. At the same time, people now judged songs or movies or novels as lifestyle accessories, not as aesthetic products. In some strange way, this became the epitome of the cool—to externalize your life as though it were one more entertainment product.

During my college years, I spent much of my free time studying music and developing my skills as a jazz pianist. Because of this obvious obsession on my part, many classmates would come up to me when they wanted to talk about their favorite records or radio stations or bands. But I soon learned that what they really wanted to talk about when they talked music was their own emerging lifestyles. When my roommate announced to me that the Sex Pistols were the greatest band in the world, he didn't mean that Johnny Rotten had a wider vocal range than Luciano Pavarotti or that Sid Vicious was a greater virtuoso than Andrés Segovia. What he really meant, even if he couldn't articulate it clearly, was that the Sex Pistols enthralled him as an extension of his own attitudes and ways of being in the world. He was part of a generation whose sense of identity and style of life was built around music. To a greater extent than ever before, popular music had now become supercharged with vague and sometimes contradictory meanings as each new generation attempted to define itself in song.

When I later started writing music criticism and books on music, I frequently ran into the same confusion. I would get caught up in puzzling and unsettling dialogues with other critics, and I would struggle to even understand what points they were trying to make. Only gradually did I discover that they were no different from my punk rock friends from college. Even music criticism had stopped being about the music and was increasingly written from the lifestyle perspective of the critic. I heard one critic boast that he took pride in recommending music to people that he knew they would never enjoy. In a previous age, such practices would have been considered the exact opposite of a critic's role. But in the brave new world of the post-sixties, when everything was about asserting the coolness of your own lifestyle, half the fun was seeing it get into a head-on collision with someone else's lifestyle. What dueling was to the nineteenth century, these lifestyle conflicts became during the 1960s and 1970s—fought with the Sex Pistols, perhaps, rather than with real pistols, but with the same attitude of assertion and desire to dominate. It is no coincidence that car radios and stereo systems got louder during these years; it was merely a small-scale version of those arms races in which technology and ego spur an inevitable escalation.

The growing influence of cool as a cultural concept was inextricably linked to this cult of lifestyle. Until people started viewing their ways of life as representing artistic styles of self-expression (that perspective so unfamiliar to my dear old mom and dad), cool could make little headway among the general population. During the Great Depression, when life was about survival, plain and simple, the words *lifestyle* and *cool* did not—indeed, could not—resonate with their current meanings. But once individuals began viewing their life choices in aesthetic and symbolic terms—as they increasingly did when the US economy in the post-Depression years gave them the financial security to do so—then coolness had room to grow and thrive. Even a purely semantic history of cool reveals this. For we will see when we examine the history of the word *cool* that its meaning changed dramatically over roughly the same period that *lifestyle* entered the vocabulary.

And just as *lifestyle* and *cool* grew up together, we will find that they also have more recently exhibited the same signs of aging and decline. The disease that afflicts both of them comes from the same point of origin: their very pervasiveness. They became trivialized as entrenched powers made them their playthings. With each passing decade, companies got smarter and better at manipulating the psychic space where our notions of lifestyle and coolness reside. But manipulation on this scale, no matter how skillfully handled, inevitably provokes a backlash. And it is now coming with a vengeance. Cool became corporatized...but only at the cost of its inner vitality.

The irony is that companies eventually made these terms into the exact opposite of what they meant back when Reich wrote *The Greening of America*. The category "lifestyle," as it is currently used in corporate boardrooms, bears no resemblance to Reich's starry-eyed vision of this concept as the nexus of self-actualization. Indeed, the "lifestyles categories" that market researchers use to pigeonhole consumers today—tossing them into groups with labels such as "strivers," "belongers," "urban tweens," and so forth—have little relation to how these people view themselves. Far from choosing their lifestyle, consumers are now assigned it by some higher power at the corporate headquarters. Most of the time, people wouldn't even recognize the name of their marketing-imposed lifestyle if it were staring them in the face on a fifty-foot-high billboard. And far from viewing lifestyle as something an individual can change and shape at will, the corporate mind-set wants to see as little change and fluidity in these categories as possible.

The history of how lifestyle was co-opted is an interesting and sobering tale, and quite relevant to our history of the rise and fall of cool. The late Arnold Mitchell is far from a household name—indeed, his name is hardly recognized even within the business community he profoundly influenced. No monument honors his achievements, and he isn't even listed in Wikipedia. But Mitchell's work from the sixties through the eighties for Stanford Research Institute (SRI), a nonprofit think tank headquartered in Menlo Park, California, would provide the key insights and techniques that would establish lifestyle analysis as a leading tool in the arsenal of corporate marketers. More than anyone else, Mitchell showed corporations how they could control and shape the very essence of cool. The lifestyle movement that Reich and others saw as a counterforce opposing corporate America would now become a method of manipulating finely segmented groups of consumers.

In the early sixties, Mitchell became increasingly fascinated by the ways in which social sciences could help businesses understand consumer spending patterns and preferences. Few business leaders at this point in time would have thought they could learn anything from anthropology—a discipline that would have seemed insufficiently hardheaded for their dollars-and-cents purposes. Yet Mitchell began working with anthropologist Kenneth J. Cooper and economist Hawkins Stern on explanatory models that might give guidance to business decisions. The first of their studies was published by SRI as *Consumer Values and Demand* in 1960.[5]

Even Mitchell would later admit that this publication had "no discernible influence on its readers, perhaps because it was ahead of its time."[6] But he persisted in a series of follow-up studies, guided by the simple but powerful premise that probing the murky area of people's inner lives—their values, their sense of self, their view of what was cool or uncool—could be the key to controlling their behavior and, above all, their wallets. The fact that Mitchell's early publications were not distributed to the general public but were restricted to an elite group of SRI clients did not help in disseminating his ideas or securing his personal fame. But no amount of secrecy could prevent his core insights from eventually spreading—so much so that *Advertising Age* would eventually credit Mitchell's development of a new psychologically rich approach to segmenting and influencing consumers as one of the breakthrough concepts of his era.

Translating sociological concepts into business strategies proved to be a challenging task. Even if one accepted the theoretical validity of Mitchell's notions, mapping the inner lives of modern-day consumers seemed more of a task for philosophy or poetry than a concrete market-research project. But the rising interest in lifestyles during the late sixties and early seventies provided the final missing piece in Mitchell's puzzle. Less than three years elapsed between Reich's *The Greening of America* and Mitchell's capitalist-driven rethinking of the lifestyle concept. In his 1973 work *Lifeways and Life-Styles*, Mitchell laid the groundwork for what, five years later, would become known as VALS (Values and Lifestyles) analysis. For SRI, this would become a major thrust of its business-consulting practice, and others would soon jump on the bandwagon.

"The first real breakthrough for VALS resulted from a competition for the Merrill Lynch account between two ad agencies, Ogilvy & Mather and Young & Rubicam," recalls Bill Guns, who worked with Mitchell at SRI.

Merrill Lynch was unhappy with their Bullish on America campaign and wanted a fresh approach. Young & Rubicam came out to meet Arnold and explained the situation to him. Arnold thought it over, then said, "Look, we all know that the target market for Merrill Lynch are the kind of people who follow the herd. But they see themselves as solitary, as individuals. So use one bull in the advertising." Young & Rubicam took Arnold's advice and built it into a memorable campaign with a bull in a china shop. After Young & Rubicam won the Merrill Lynch account, Ogilvy & Mather signed up for VALS the next day. From then on, even if you weren't going to apply the VALS approach, you needed to know what it said—because someone else would.[7]

Mitchell would eventually identify nine modern lifestyles, the first detailed blueprint for marketing *inside* people's heads. He created a schema based on painstaking statistical analysis—a wide range of participants were asked a battery of more than eight hundred questions that he believed encompassed the full range of modern American life. Understanding these lifestyle patterns offered nothing less than a road map to the psyches of contemporary consumers. Traditional demographics looked at people's age or gender or education levels, but these had only limited predictive power and offered little help to those trying to influence attitudes and behavior patterns. But the Values and Lifestyles approach cut through the noise of the marketplace to essential mechanisms undergirding how people thought and believed and acted.

Here are Mitchell's nine original lifestyles:

Survivors: With their poor education and low income, these individuals devote much of their energy to basic issues of survival and security. Many suffer from health issues. They tend to be suspicious, distrustful, and prone to depression. Their worldview is bleak and pessimistic.

Sustainers: These individuals also have low incomes. But, unlike Survivors, they have not given in to despair. They work hard, often at low-paying jobs, and take pride in making each dollar go a long way. They are aggressive, combative, and sometimes quite street-smart. They have low satisfaction with life, but have a high need for social status and want to feel accepted (or even admired) by their peers and neighbors.

Belongers: This group is the backbone of middle-class America and was the largest lifestyle category at the time Mitchell began his work on lifestyles. Belongers are a force of stability in communities and churches, and they exemplify traditional values. They tend to have average levels of income and education and live in small towns or in the country. They are patriotic, family-oriented, moral (sometimes puritanical), and sociable. They do not view themselves as sophisticated or interested in experimentation. They are often nostalgic and view the past as the good ol' days.

Emulators: Emulators are ambitious and fairly successful, but they shape their goals and purchasing decisions by imitating those who are even more successful. They tend to be younger and hold jobs that require higher skills, but despite their above-average income they are often in debt. They engage in conspicuous consumption, spending on things that will impress others. They follow movies, fashion, and contemporary trends, which often shape their worldview, but their personal reality rarely lives up to these romanticized notions. As a result, this group is often dissatisfied and feels rejected. Their inner lives may be hollow, as they follow trends set by others.

Achievers: These high-income, achievement-oriented individuals thrive in the current system—and for the most part, they also run it. Many lawyers, doctors, and executives belong to this elite group. Achievers are mostly satisfied with their lives and are not rebellious or counterculture (although their children often are). They live comfortably and in many ways set the standards for other groups (such as Emulators).

I-Am-Mes: These individuals tend to be younger, often students or living with parents. Their sense of self is still in development, and as a result I-Am-Mes can be volatile and unpredictable, easygoing one day and aggressive the next. They are often flamboyant, conspicuous, and assertive, although not always in predictable ways. These individuals have high levels of energy and enthusiasm, but their choices—as consumers, voters, and community members—are still in flux. Many I-Am-Mes will move into other lifestyle groups in the coming years.

Experientials: These individuals are quick to jump into the new and different, often with a boldness that leaves others breathless. They do things with vigor and focus, but often with little concern for the norms or expectations of their peers. Experientials are well-educated, relatively young, and have enough income to allow them to engage in everything from hang gliding to wine tasting. They can be spiritual or delve into recreational drugs, but whatever they do the intensity of the experience is of paramount importance to them.

Societally Conscious: These individuals come closest to the vision of lifestyles as articulated by the sixties generation. They are deeply concerned with social and political issues, paying close attention to current events, trends, and movements. They are often important members of their communities, but sometime participate in an aggressive, confrontational manner. Yet they, too, are consumers, often discerning ones, paying attention to packaging, contents, place of origin, and other factors. Many are highly educated with above-average incomes.

Integrateds: This last lifestyle category was both the smallest and most difficult for Mitchell to describe. The Integrateds were capable of blending in with community and groups and sometimes led and directed others in ways that were far from obvious. They were mature and balanced, capable of playing various roles within different contexts. Their political leanings were often less predictable than the liberal Societally Conscious or conservative Belongers, but this did not mean that Integrateds were not interested in social issues. Often they had deeply held values and opinions that influenced their behavior. However (and of paramount importance for our purposes), these individuals were not jumping on trends or overly concerned with current fads and fashions. Mitchell thought that this group would play an increasingly decisive role in the functioning of future society.[8]

These nine lifestyles moved from the needs-driven behavior of the first two groups (Survivors, Sustainers), to the outward focus of the next three groups (Belongers, Emulators, Achievers), to the inner-directed behavior of the next three (I-Am-Mes, Experientials, Societally Conscious), to the final category, Integrateds, which combined elements of outer- and inner-driven behavior.

For each of these cohorts, Mitchell assessed what they bought, what credit cards they used, what magazines they read, what television programs they watched, and where they shopped, and he collected reams of other data that might prove useful to corporate marketers. SRI also began to take the VALS approach overseas and was able to tell its clients that Americans were more likely to be Belongers than the French, that Germany was a country of Sustainers, that Sweden had more than its fair share of Achievers, that Italy had a large contingent of Societally Conscious, and other such insights.

The last group, Integrateds, proved to be the most fascinating and troublesome for the SRI researchers—and also the group that will help us understand why cool would eventually lose its luster. Put simply, the Integrateds were the most difficult to address from a marketing perspective. The power of VALS analysis derived from its ability to identify the right marketing formula for each of these groups, and even from the snapshot summaries, one can see how sales pitches would need to be adapted to influence Experientials rather than, for example, Belongers or Emulators. Each of these had some hot button that, if pressed, could convince the lifestyle cohorts that a company or product or brand was the new cool thing. But the Integrateds were, for the most part, marketing resistant. They didn't imitate others or strive to keep up with the Joneses; they weren't predictable in their allegiances or impulsive in their purchasing. "The Integrateds pose a particular problem," Mitchell lamented at one point in his 1983 book, *The Nine American Lifestyles*, "because to date we have not developed a computational way to identify them."[9] The Integrateds were especially difficult to track on the basis of consumption-driven measurements so favored by marketers, in which people are defined by their spending patterns.

To make matters worse, even as far back as the seventies, Mitchell's data suggested that these Integrateds were also the fastest-growing lifestyle group. They would become an increasingly influential force in the coming decades. And their sheer numbers were only half the story. There was also a large group of what Mitchell called pre-Integrateds: members of other lifestyle groups who were moving, at various speeds, toward a more Integrated life-style. Although Mitchell believed that only 2 percent of Americans were Integrated, *more than half of the people he interviewed* saw themselves as part of the Integrated category. This was the lifestyle to which they clearly aspired, even if they weren't there yet. Mitchell didn't go so far as to say that extrapolating this trend for another generation would indicate the looming death of the cool…but, in fact, this is precisely what has happened. This still tiny (in the seventies and eighties) but rapidly growing group of marketing-immune consumers were sowing the seeds for the phenomenon that is the subject of this book.

The more closely Mitchell examined lifestyle trends, the more he saw the coming bad news for marketers. As early as 1976, Mitchell, working in conjunction with Duane Elgin, identified a surprising trend that the researchers labeled "voluntary simplicity." Previous generations had sometimes lived simple, meager lives, but this was usually a matter of necessity, not choice. Social thinker

Richard Gregg had coined the term *voluntary simplicity* back in
1936—but Gregg was an eccentric, a fringe figure who had quit
his law career to hang out with Gandhi. Certainly he was not a
role model or indicator of what average folks might think or do.
But forty years later, a meaningful segment of the population was
opting for lives that were outwardly simple but inwardly rich. These
individuals, Elgin and Mitchell noted, were rejecting consumption
as an end in itself and building their lives instead around personal
growth, community, and a concern for environmental issues that
ran counter to the materialistic tenor of the times.

This was more than just a fleeting trend driven by hippies and
rebellious youths, the researchers noted. It was not just an out-
growth of the back-to-nature movement. They predicted, with great
accuracy, that this was a philosophy of life that would cut through
the divisions of urban and rural, young and old, and the other
standard demographics. The authors made bold claims: "Voluntary
Simplicity is important because it may foreshadow a major transformation in the goals and values of the United States in the coming
decades."[10]

In time, SRI was forced to revamp its VALS categories and,
after Mitchell's death, even eliminated the pesky Integrateds from
their analyses. Today, VALS has eight lifestyles—not nine—and the
Integrateds are no longer part of the schema. Nor are the adherents
of voluntary simplicity represented in current-day VALS studies.
But the problems Mitchell identified have not gone away. In truth,
they remain the key challenges facing the legions of marketers who,
every day in every consumer-product industry, use lifestyle analysis to influence our sense of what is cool, desirable, fashionable,
necessary. Like a population that has survived some viral disease
and is now immune to its ravages, the Integrateds, pre-Integrateds,
and advocates of voluntary simplicity have built up a resistance to
these corporate mind games. And instead of jumping on the latest
cool trend, these increasingly influential folks are already on to
something else.

In the coming chapters, we will try to identify what that something else might be. But even at this stage, Mitchell's predictions of
a future dominated by Integrated consumers and those opting for
voluntary simplicity—predictions that even his heirs at SRI have
tried to sweep under the rug in favor of more marketing-friendly
findings—help us understand many otherwise puzzling trends and
events of recent years. What at first blush seem to be anomalies
are in fact explained by the failure of corporate decision makers
to adapt to an environment in which more and more people resist

marketing, do not jump on trends or fads, and have frequently moved beyond the cool.

How else to explain that dirty little secret of the marketing profession—the collapse in brand power during the new millennium? This was the real Y2K problem facing corporations...but few of them are paying attention even now. In a complete reversal of everything taught in business school, advertising is not only losing its clout, but is increasingly perceived by consumers as a sign of a company's weakness, not its strength. The Wall Street Journal has even coined the term *logo-phobic* and puzzles over affluent "shoppers who are moving away from recognizable labels in search of something else."[11] Isn't the logo the ultimate sign of a brand's value? Why would a wealthy shopper, who can afford anything, want to dispense with it?

But even the mass market is now blocking out the incessant branding messages in the media. In October 2004, Coca-Cola hired a market-research firm to test the public's recognition of its advertising slogan "Real!," which it had been flogging for eighteen months at a cost of tens of millions of dollars. But only 5 percent of customers could recall this simple phrase. Yet Coca-Cola fared better than Burger King, whose slogan "It's Better Here" tested with *0 percent* unaided recognition.

Zero percent? How can that be possible? Even more striking, this collapse in ad-driven brands is taking place at the same time other companies (Google, Starbucks, Amazon, eBay, Costco, and the like) are becoming dominant players in their industries with almost no television or radio advertising. Is it possible that *not* advertising is helping to build their brand? And why are the companies with the most heavily marketed brands increasingly forced to create new ones? Brand fragmentation is everywhere. Take a look at the potato chip section of your supermarket and try to count the options. How can a company spend hundreds of millions of dollars building a megabrand only to decide a short while later that it needs to start another new one from scratch? Or how can we explain the rapidly spreading trend of well-known companies working to *hide* their brand names in their fastest-growing businesses? How have microbreweries, without any brand power, been able to gain share against megabrands such as Budweiser and Miller? In 2007, the US beer market grew 1.4 percent, while microbreweries showed a 21 percent increase. This disparity in growth rate has been evident for more than a decade. Meanwhile, Anheuser-Busch spends in excess of $15 million per year just on Super Bowl ads. Could it be that consumers increasingly want the beer that is *not* advertised during the Super Bowl? What a strange idea—at least until you understand the psychographic underpinnings of this shift. Welcome to the new millennium, Mr. Brewmeister!

One could cite many similar examples—apparent paradoxes that seem to prove that the more a company spends to be cool, the less success it has in achieving that goal. Look at the results when Starbucks announced in late 2007 that it intended to ramp up its spending on advertising. For the longest time, Starbucks spent only 1 or 2 percent of sales on advertising, compared to Coca-Cola, which routinely invests more than 10 percent of revenue into these brand-building activities. The company now proposed to change this approach and increase its marketing investment. A smart move? Savvy observers saw this as bad news for the brand. During the six months following the announcement, Starbucks shares on the NASDAQ fell by 34 percent—at a time when competitors Peet's and Green Mountain Coffee Roasters were growing their businesses and their stock prices.

When these fiascos happen, the advertising firm is fired, a new head of marketing is brought in, or the company pays for an expensive brand retooling. Chief marketing officers have the most precarious jobs in the executive suite these days—the average one is replaced every twenty-three months at the top consumer-products companies (compared to fifty-four months for the CEO). But the real story here isn't that Burger King picked a bad slogan or Budweiser needs a better agency. A lifestyle shift in modern society is now accelerating and creating a large cadre of smart, affluent people who are resistant to mass-marketed notions of coolness. Sometimes they are merely indifferent to the coolocracy imposed by corporate America, occasionally they are overtly hostile, and a few (but growing number) are so cussedly anticool that they will seek out the exact opposite of what marketers and media are proclaiming as the cool flavor of the month. For the most part, these folks are quietly doing their own thing, calibrating their lives, not their lifestyles, according to their own deeply held values and views.

When *USA Today* ran an article in early 2009 about a couple who, under severe financial pressures, gave up their credit cards, satellite TV, restaurant dining, and other luxuries and moved to a forty-acre farm, the paper labeled the family "economic survivalists" who were the victims of bad times. Hundreds of readers responded with comments praising the couple and refusing to see them as victims. "They are right on the mark." "They look pretty happy to me." "I don't know if this is so much survivalism as a return to common sense." "This is not really an 'offbeat' story. These are REAL Americans."[12] A few days later, Peggy Noonan wrote about this same couple in *The Wall Street Journal*, suggesting that they were part of a larger trend. She noted the unexpected increase in sales of vegetable seeds and transplants—up 30 percent year-on-year—and similar upticks in the purchase of sewing products, canning equipment, and other back-to-basics items. Noonan mulled the possibility that this shift is more than just a response to economic pressures: "Bland affluence is over," she concludes, and even speculated that this new naturalism might lead to "fewer facelifts and browlifts, less Botox, less dyed hair."[13] Could it be?

Yes, we have now even reached a point where there is a backlash against the very concept of lifestyle. In an acerbic commentary on *Fresh Air* in July 2006, Geoffrey Nunberg attacked the concept of a gay lifestyle—no, not because he is homophobic, but because he feels that the word *lifestyle* is demeaning to gays. Nunberg recognized that some people object to this phrase because it implies there is only one gay lifestyle, and thus ignores the underlying diversity, but this, he claimed, misses the real point. "The real affront is simply in using *lifestyle* in the first place," he asserted, "as if homosexuality were just another choice like deciding to get a mullet or build a backyard hot tub." For Nunberg, the modern-day obsession with lifestyles is simply "exaggerating the significance of shallow differences."[14]

Nunberg is not alone in his perceptions. Today, when people get caught up in the cool new video game or website or television show, their friends tell them, "Get a life." You don't hear them say, "Get a lifestyle." What a revealing phrase! And I suspect that "Get a life" has become such a popular edict because it cuts to the quick of the marketing- and media-driven fraudulence surrounding us. It is the quintessential postcool put-down...*Get a life!*

In fact, the phrase reminds me of something my parents would have said if they had spent any time thinking up clever repartee. It turns out that those uncool cats, the survivors of the Great Depression who knew nothing about lifestyles but quite a lot about living, were actually ahead of the times. Postcool is, to a surprising extent, coming to resemble the precool days of yore. For all of us, the time may be coming very soon when we will be expected to put our cool lifestyle accessories aside and instead focus on...getting a life.

How Cool Became So

If we take the temperature of the word *cool*, we find that its meaning has changed markedly over the years. There was a time, not long ago, when the word wasn't quite so cool. As the last chapter suggests, its shifting significations are not unrelated to the growing importance of the concept of lifestyle. During the years between the introduction of the word *lifestyle* into the English language in 1929 and its acceptance as a mantra for self-actualization in the 1960s, the word *cool* was also reconfigured, taking on its current meaning as a label for fashionable hipness—a signification that, over time, would expand to encompass nothing less than a personality style and even a way of life.

This correlation should not surprise us. The cult of cool helped build the lifestyle revolution and vice versa. The growing tendency of individuals to view their ways of existence as a lifestyle (and not just a life) made them eager worshippers at the shrine of coolness. As I pointed out, it is hard to comprehend the workings of social life during the last half of the twentieth century without understanding how aesthetic and lifestyle concepts were becoming blurred and jumbled together. In the closing decades of the century, almost every decision a person made, from the first thing in the morning with the choice of wardrobe, toiletries, and so forth to turning off the television or CD player before falling asleep at night, was charged with symbolic lifestyle resonance. These decisions were not simply indicators of what I *did*, not just evidence of what I *owned*; to a greater and greater extent, they defined who I was as a person. I have a lifestyle, therefore I am.

It is hard for most of us to realize how recently all this came about. Despite my parents' total lack of cool attitude, they were light-years ahead of my grandparents and great-grandparents. At least Mom and Dad could exercise *some* control over how they dressed, what music they heard, what entertainments they watched. Their forebears, in contrast, were born into social milieus that tended to dictate these things. Only a small ruling elite could exercise real choice on any meaningful scale, and even the choices of the ruling class were made not so much with regard to concepts of lifestyle or hipness, but rather to communicate and enforce the privileges and status of class and wealth. The king does not wear the crown just because it's shiny and looks good. Nor does he change it for a hat just because a more fashionable style of headgear has arrived on the scene.

The shift in the meaning of *cool* is all the more surprising when you consider that, if you go back far enough, the label was almost never used as a term of praise. Since the dawn of the written word, most languages equate words signifying cold temperatures with emotional aloofness and indifference. In fact, a linguist once told me that this metaphorical equation of standoffish or hostile behavior with the downward shift on the thermometer is true in *every* language—a sweeping claim that, if true, forces one to ponder the deep psychic valence of coolness. In any event, the sheer number of pejorative wintry words that have entered into our vocabulary of personal description is quite striking. *Cool, frigid, chilly, frosty, cold, icy*—these adjectives can also be applied to people, not just meteorological phenomena, and rarely with warm intentions. When Shakespeare has Cardinal Beaufort warn King Henry VI that his actions will make his supporters "cool in zeal unto your grace," or describes a woman as "a cold fish" in *A Winter's Tale*, or when Milton, describing the eviction of Adam and Eve from the Garden of Eden, explains how "from wrath more cool / Came the mild Judge," these poets are keeping true to the time-honored spirit of such words. According to the emotional weather vane we keep in our psyches, cool is bad and hot is good.

There are clearly deep-seated reasons for this subliminal relationship of temperatures and emotions. Recent research conducted by Chen-Bo Zhong and Geoffrey J. Leonardelli found that people asked to estimate the temperature in the testing lab gave answers four degrees lower, on average, if they were first required to recall a past situation of social exclusion. The researchers also discovered that subjects who were given the cold shoulder in a ball-tossing exercise—excluded from most of the throwing—had a higher preference for warm foods afterward.[1] Other studies have confirmed this correlation between social integration and temperature. Just holding a cup of a hot drink in your hand can increase your sympathetic feelings for the people around you. Given this subliminal connection, it should come as little surprise that chilly words reflect aloof attitudes. This correlation was reflected in everyday language until the middle of the twentieth century when, in a puzzling turnabout, *cool* reversed course and became a term of praise and affirmation.

When *cool* first started to develop its slang meaning, the negative aspect of the term no doubt added to its resonance. We find many examples from the 1820s onward in which the term suggests insolence or impudence, a sauciness that pushes beyond acceptable everyday behavior.[2] When Francis Durivage and George Burnham employ it in their slang dialogue for *Stray Subjects* (1848), the reader finds few hints of the modern, positive connotation in their character's outburst: "You are the coolest specimen of a genuine scamp that it has ever been my ill luck to meet with." In other usages from this era, we hear references to "cool scoundrels" or find the adjective applied to a prisoner or gunman or even a rattlesnake. In the 1920s, we find *cool* morphing from an adjective into a menacing verb, but with scarcely any more indication of its later positive tone in this new application. It now signifies killing someone or knocking them unconscious. We read about "coolin' a cop" or find Hemingway writing, "I'd like to cool you, you rummy fake." But cool wasn't always bad, even in its nineteenth-century form; as early as the 1840s, to "take it cool" conveys an unruffled and relaxed demeanor, certainly not in the stylish modern sense, but more in the manner of a soldier who keeps his head amidst the heat of battle.

The modern sense of *cool*, as modified by African American culture, would carry a sense of fashionability and sophisticated demeanor. Yet, given the prevalence of the word today, it is surprising how late in the game this new usage became prevalent. I was dumbfounded to learn that *cool* does not appear in Cab Calloway's *Cat-ologue: A Hepsters Dictionary*, first published in 1938. In his ambitious lexicon, the Hi-De-Ho Man—as Cab was known in those days—taught the squares (defined by Calloway as "an unhep person") a host of useful modifiers unknown to Shakespeare and Chaucer. Here we find *foxy, groovy, hip, dicty, hincty, righteous*, and *zoot*. Here we learn to use tried-and-true conversation starters, such as "Do you collar this jive?" or "Why don't we truck on down to the gin mill?" But Cab, probably the coolest cat on the planet, circa 1938, never mentions *cool*. Huh?

Nor does the word show up as an entry in *The Slim Gaillard Vout-o-Reenee Dictionary* of hipster slang from mid-1940s.[3] It is also absent from the lexicon included in *Dan Burley's Original Handbook of Harlem Jive*, from 1944. Yet Burley is apparently famil-

iar with the modern usage, since we find the word showing up elsewhere in the book, for example in a caption on page 101 describing
a "Portrait of a Cool Stud Hyping his Chick." Then, three years
later—not long before Miles Davis's first *Birth of the Cool* recordings—we finally find *cool* defined in Marcus Hanna Boulware's *Jive
and Slang of Students in Negro Colleges* as "neatly dressed," and *cool
papa* explicated as a "nonchalant fellow."

Here, literally at the start of the baby boom, we are finally on the
solid ground of coolness as a modern fashion statement encompassing
attitude and attire, the right demeanor married to the right accessories. We should not be surprised that the new meaning, like the attitude it describes, comes from the African American community—we
will find this connection between coolness and blackness again and
again in our survey. But within a few years of Boulware's lexicon, the
words and behavior patterns of cool would enter white mainstream
society with a vengeance. The modern Age of Cool had begun.

But if *cool* was late to arrive on the scene as a term of approval,
many of the philosophical elements that contributed to its ethos had
been brewing for a long time. Historians of cool have been inge-
nious in seeking out the roots of this underlying philosophy. Nick
Southgate, in his article "Coolhunting with Aristotle," will tell you
that the Greek philosopher was the first cool cat, having sketched
out a laid-back and balanced approach to life in *The Nicomachean
Ethics.*[4] Others look to West Africa, where Yoruban and Ibo belief
systems stressed restraint, conciliation, and nonconfrontational
ways of interaction that prefigure the later currents of cool. Scholar
Robert Farris Thompson sees coolness in the "purse-lipped forms
of African figural sculpture," as well as in rituals, linguistic usages,
and habits of personal hygiene and social interaction. His relentless
sleuthing even identified a fifteenth-century African king, ruler of
the Benin Empire from 1440 to 1473, who was honored with the
title of Ewuare—which Thompson conveniently translates as "It
is cool" (or, as I prefer to translate it, "How cool is that?," which I
think is the perfect title for any emperor)—for his successful efforts
to bring peace to a war-torn region.[5]

But the twentieth-century philosophy of cool would prove to be
more than just a matter of attitude and behavior. In truth, it eventually boiled down to how one was perceived by others. Coolness,
even more than beauty, is inevitably in the eye of the beholder.
Your attire and accessories, your language and pose, are cool only
to the extent that others buy into their hipness. Here we come to
grips with both the supreme elegance of the cool and the cause of
its underlying neurosis and ultimate instability as a way of life. Put

simply, if you cannot get others to accept your cool status, the game is over. You can adopt the strangest garb or lingo you can find, but you will merely be an oddball. As comedian Russell Brand quips, "Without fame, this haircut could be mistaken for mental illness."

Coolness, to a frustrating degree, is outside your control—it only comes when others laud your most righteous hairdo and start following in your wake. The true masters of cool know this. They have emerged as the hippest cats by shaping how others perceive their coolness. For this angle on cool, we can't look to Aristotle or African sculpture. A more appropriate founding father is, rather, the Renaissance courtier Baldassare Castiglione, born in 1478—five years after the end of the reign of King Ewuare.

In his influential *Il Cortegiano*, or *The Book of the Courtier*, Castiglione prizes what he calls *sprezzatura*—the art of doing difficult things, but making them look easy. "Avoid affectation in every way possible," he writes. "Conceal all art and make whatever is done or said appear to be without effort and almost without any thought about it." The courtier's style—relaxed, confident, without sweat or bother—is essential to the overall effect. The key here is the emphasis on appearance, which is now even more important than the underlying reality. With *sprezzatura*, something is always concealed, but elegantly so.[6]

Then again, Castiglione should not be confused with his contemporary Machiavelli, who practiced a more manipulative variant on the same theme. The deception of *sprezzatura* is a pleasing one; it cultivates its mystery in order to make it enticing and beguiling—much like the smile of the Mona Lisa. Nor is it coincidence that da Vinci was painting his famous portrait at the same time that Castiglione was developing his concept of *sprezzatura*—cool is never created by an individual working in isolation, like some kind of scientific breakthrough done in a lab, but is always the result of a group of like-minded people operating with similar views. Coolness may put on a pose of haughty individualism, but, in reality, it is the ultimate in groupthink.

It is not a great distance from *Mona Lisa* to Miles Davis—although one always smiled and the other was famous for never doing so—from Renaissance *sprezzatura* to the modern sense of cool. In both, we find lingering traces of the original, pejorative sense of cool as emotionally distanced, but superimposed on this is an aura of skill and fluency, of quiet competence. But above all, we have the new, modern twist, the idealization of image, and a deeper awareness that what is polished on the surface may coexist with more complex layers beneath. The image coyly hints at the nuances below, but never reveals them completely, always keeps something in reserve. This simple fact explains much of the allure of cool. This proved to be a useful formula for Renaissance court life, as demonstrated by the tremendous popularity of Castiglione's book, and for the stars of cool jazz in the 1950s. In the second half of the twentieth century, *sprezzatura* became a lifestyle and attitude for the masses.

Inevitably, other strains of thought and ways of behaving blended with or countered the appealing cult of *sprezzatura*. The traditional reserve of the English upper class—the so-called stiff upper lip—represented a different solution to the same problem of reconciling the difficulties of the inner emotional life with the need for a more decorous appearance on the surface. Ironically, the earliest usage of the idiomatic expression "stiff upper lip" is traced to the United States, not England, where it shows up in *The Massachusetts Spy* from June 14, 1815. It is perhaps worth noting that the first slang usage of *cool*, indicating impudence or brashness, appears in the English periodical *The Spy* from this same period. Of course, during this era, the cult of Romanticism was spreading in both Britain and the United States and reflected the growing obsession of the leading thinkers and artists with the conflict between the turbulence of the inner life with the constraints of social norms and expectations. To some degree, Romanticism set up the problem to which cool would be the solution.

Thus we have a continuum, a range of responses to the growing awareness of the divergence between appearance and reality. At the far extreme, we have the example of Jean-Jacques Rousseau, who let it all hang out, in modern parlance, offering in his *Confessions* (1782) such honesty about his basest behavior and strangest habits that readers could hardly understand why he didn't keep these tawdry facts to himself. At the other end of the spectrum, we have the unreal refinement of royalty and the highest spheres of the ruling class, where everything is a polished image, giving no sense of the reality below, and even the apparently spontaneous gestures of noblesse oblige or self-sacrifice for king and country are carefully cultivated in response to social norms and expectations. Precariously balanced in the middle is the tone of behavior that we would come to know as cool, that delicate balance between revealing and concealing, authenticity and artifice, all infused with a dose of *La Gioconda* mystery.

The black community, which would play the key role in disseminating the cool into mainstream society, needed to develop its own ways of navigating through the especially tricky and dangerous conflict between inner and outer imperatives it constantly encountered in the New World. Where on this continuum would black Americans land? Would they be like Rousseau and let it all hang out? Be brutally honest in expressing what they thought and did? Hardly! Perhaps a few brave or foolish souls did just that, but many of them were no doubt punished, maimed, or killed as a result. Instead, most African Americans learned from a very young age to keep their own counsel, learned that what they said or did could and would be held against them—and usually *not* in a court of law.

Would African Americans go, then, to the other extreme, and adopt the stiff upper lip of the British? Would they hold it as a mark of pride and honor that they could withstand the slings and arrows of outrageous fortune without making the smallest complaint? Would they build an attitude and way of life around meek acceptance of the cards they had been dealt? Certainly some tried to do just that—but most no doubt felt that this abject pose was as unacceptable as the Rousseauian option. Perhaps a nobility and upper class could find comfort in quietly accepting the downsides of a system they controlled, created, and exploited for their own use. But when you were the exploited one, when you were forcibly taken from your homeland and made to toil and serve against your will in settings not of your own choosing…there was no honor in upholding such a system with quiet fortitude and humble submission to fate.

Inevitably African Americans needed a middle ground—but one that (paradoxically) could embrace both extremes. You would need to be a rare genius to solve this problem. How could you speak your mind while appearing to remain quiet? How could you express deep inner emotions with honesty while apparently holding them in check? How could you assert your individuality while living in a community that demanded the utmost conformity and subservience? How could you exist outside the scope of oppressive social rules and imperatives while also following them to the letter?

The worldview and ways of behaving that grew out of this need to embrace paradox were what would eventually become known as *the cool*. They borrowed from the insights of *sprezzatura*, especially in its acceptance of a duality between appearance and reality, and an understanding that no strain or anguish could show up on the surface level. But black Americans added elements of their own, some drawn from African patterns of behavior, where attitudes of conciliation, avoidance of conflict within the community, and an easygoing affability were nurtured and encouraged. On top of this, new ingredients were layered that were unique responses to the American scene.

In particular, African Americans became masters of a verbal fluency that allowed them to navigate between the rigidly imposed demands of socially acceptable discourse and their own pressing need to circumscribe their social situation in their own words and phrases. In time, this rich, poetic—and often cryptic—method of self-expression became known as "signifying." Henry Louis Gates Jr., drawing on Roger Abrahams, defines it as

> the ability to talk with great innuendo, to carp, cajole, needle and lie. It can mean in other instances the propensity to talk around a subject, never quite coming to the point. It can mean making fun of a person or situation. Also it can denote speaking with the hands and eyes, and in this respect encompasses a whole complex of expressions and gestures.[7]

Gates traces this cultural pattern back to the African and Caribbean figure of the trickster in his various incarnations—and the list of adjectives he offers as descriptions of this mythic archetype serves essentially as a point-by-point summary of the cool personality: "A partial list of these qualities might include individuality, satire, parody, irony, magic, indeterminacy, open-endedness, ambiguity, sexuality, chance, uncertainty, disruption and reconciliation, betrayal and loyalty, closure and disclosure, encasement and rupture."[8] Those familiar with jazz might recognize Miles Davis in this laundry list of attributes. A beatnik would see Jack Kerouac. A film buff might think of Jack Nicholson. The modern cool was, in short, the trickster in updated garb, suitable for the mass media of the second half of the twentieth century.

When language is translated into signifying, all the normal laws of semantics, of cause and effect, are transformed. Gates offers the example of a group of black high school students in North Carolina who, dismayed over the rigidity of standardized achievement tests, devised one more to their own liking. They convinced a group of employees at publisher McGraw-Hill to take this exam, and these custodians of the written word all received Cs and Ds. A typical question: "Who is buried in Grant's tomb?" The correct answer, true to the dictates of signifying: "Your mama." Gates, in his characteristically dry manner, adds, "It is difficult to explain why this response is so funny."[9]

When cool captured the American imagination in the fifties, this duality would come to the fore. Cool would be embedded in a series of signifying paradoxes. It would reveal while keeping things hidden. It would be emotionally involved while maintaining its distance. It would be obsessively focused on style and attitude while always showing its total disdain for these same superficial attributes. And even when it amused, it was sometimes difficult to explain why it was so funny.

No wonder cool came to conquer the world. An approach this flexible, this adaptive to every situation, was a sure winner at the midpoint of the American Century. In the 1950s, everyone was dishing up some new recipe for self-actualization for the general public, but all the others—from Dr. Norman Vincent Peale's positive thinking to L. Ron Hubbard's Dianetics—were ninety-eight-pound weaklings at the beach compared to this new, slick approach that worked for everybody, high and low.

Were you rich? Well, you needed to hone that cool image to match your bank account. Were you poor? Well, my friend, you needed a dose of cool even more than Mr. Moneybags. "Cool is about making a dollar out of fifteen cents," Donnell Alexander has astutely explained in his provocative essay "Cool Like Me: Are Black People Cooler Than White People?" Cool is "an industry of style that everyone in the world can use. It's finding the essential soul while being essentially lost."[10]

Were you beautiful? Then cool for you was like water for a mermaid, the medium through which you swam to show off your finer points. Were you plain or even ugly? Well, cool was your best friend, because with the right attitude and accoutrements you could rise above that pug nose, that double chin. Were you happy? Then cool would make you happier. Were you sad or desperate or resentful? Well, cool could even turn that into a type of allure, making angry young men into something chic and happening.

The American fixation with coolness may seem like a sign of shallowness—until you realize how much this attitude fit in with the essence of the national character. After all, the American dream was all about breaking through the limitations of class, birth, personal history, family—all the baggage that kept the Old World in thrall to the powers that be. Perhaps America didn't always live up to its aspirations. Yes, there were individuals and groups shut out from its promises. But coolness was, in some odd way, the truest embodiment of what America dangled in front of its huddled masses. It represented the possibility that you could radically reinvent your life, achieve some level of personal heroism and respect, without anyone caring about your family tree or the balance in your checking account or what schools you attended. Cool was the great equalizer. And if you doubted it, just look at the icons of cool—blacks and beatniks and bohemians and a bunch of other folks who were at the bottom of the heap and rose to the top...through sheer hipness. How cool is that? Ewuare!

This was exactly the message that Americans wanted to hear after surviving the Great Depression and World War II. For postwar society, cool was a panacea, a secular sermon with more happy endings than the beatitudes. The cool shall be comforted *and* have their fill *and* inherit the earth. And look very stylish in the process.

But a change like this needed role models, and not the usual suspects. Which cool icons could you find to emulate on Main Street in Anytown, USA? Mom and Dad? The mayor or the police chief? The minister? Teachers at the schools? None of these fit the bill. Where do you turn when you want to leave the old ways behind and embrace something cool? What fills the gap when you leave small-town life behind? If you are a farm-raised boy in, say, Davenport, Iowa, and you want to break out and start a new life, who is your role model?

One of the premises of this book is the (perhaps surprising) assertion that over the course of the fifties and sixties, a whole generation started acting like jazz musicians. Of course, they may not have realized that this was where their attitude and style came from—for the most part, they thought they were making it up for themselves as they went along. (That's a very jazzy idea right there, huh?) These folks may never have purchased a jazz record or gone to a jazz club. They might not have been able to tell a blue note from a bluebird. Yet, as we trace the genealogy of the new cool and counterculture ethos, we find an interesting family tree filled in with the names of sax players and trumpeters, jive artists and cool cats, jazz musicians who would have been surprised to learn that their most pervasive impact on society had nothing to do with how they soloed on "I Got Rhythm" or hit high notes on the horn.

If you ask a panel of jazz experts to pick the three performers who, purely from a musical perspective, created the cool jazz aesthetic, they would likely come back with these names: Bix Beiderbecke, Lester Young, and Miles Davis. But here is an odd coincidence—or is it really? If you ask for a list of three jazz musicians whose attitude and lifestyles best prefigured the later cool behavior patterns that fascinated mainstream society, you would probably come up with the same three names. And here is the most peculiar coincidence of them all. If you were ranking the strangest, most off-the-wall musical artists of the era, these three would all be candidates for top honors.

Even by the loose and tolerant standards of the jazz world, Bix, Lester, and Miles were eccentrics and oddballs, operating far beyond the norms of what constituted acceptable behavior. Many who knew them were nonplussed or intimidated by them, and even their closest friends found them puzzling and sometimes dangerous to be around. In an art form that prided itself on going beyond the everyday, they were the most out-cats of all.

Fast-forward a few decades, and these same three outliers on the bell curve become the norm, the role models for everybody else? Whoa, how did that happen? Let's find out.

The Progenitor of Cool: Bix Beiderbecke

4

Long before it had a name, a cool attitude thrived in the jazz world. But even here—or especially here—the paradox at the very core of cool made itself felt. When jazz first captivated the American public during the 1920s, the most common adjective used to describe this music was *hot*. Fans spoke of "hot jazz" or sometimes left out the *jazz* entirely and just called it "hot music." No matter, everybody knew what they were talking about. Louis Armstrong's most famous recording bands of the era were known as the Hot Five and the Hot Seven. Jelly Roll Morton called his band the Red Hot Peppers. Even overseas, when the first great European jazz band was formed by guitarist Django Reinhardt and violinist Stéphane Grappelli, the group rose to fame as the Quintette du Hot Club de France.

How could something so hot also be so cool? This music seemed to exist on two levels. There was a surface level, all fire and energy, a sound and fury so direct and unapologetic, so in-your-face, that all other styles of musical performance of that era seemed restrained by comparison. Yet below this loomed a hidden level, an interior landscape, a reserve behind the hot that imparted an aura of mystery, of cool aloofness to the whole proceeding. This is signifying at its highest pitch—contrary meanings coexisting in the discourse of African American culture, even when put on the stage as commercial entertainment and polished art. As we shall see, paradox is always at the root of modern cool, and this particular one is the most important of all. It stands out as the alluring contradiction that set everything in motion.

From the start, the white commentators who tried to come to grips with jazz sensed—and were fascinated by—this duality, the cool behind the hot. As early as 1919, when few recordings of African American jazz had been released on the market, Swiss conductor Ernst-Alexandre Ansermet managed to hear London

performances by the Southern Syncopated Orchestra, which featured the great New Orleans clarinetist Sidney Bechet. Ansermet
was awestruck by what he encountered, and in the article he wrote
for *La Revue Romande*—the first attempt by a serious musical mind
to write a real critical appreciation of jazz—he touched on precisely
the enigma of this hidden dimension in the music.

This band's music represented, in Ansermet's words, a "mys-
terious new world," and though the conductor tried to analyze the
songs played by the Southern Syncopated Orchestra, he was forced
to admit that "it is not the material that makes Negro music, it is
the spirit." He reached for a clumsy mixed metaphor combining the
cool and the hot in his attempt to explicate meanings only partially
glimpsed: "It seems as if a great wind is passing over a forest or as
if a door is suddenly opened on a wild orgy." Yet Ansermet did not
shy away from grand pronouncements. He proclaimed that Bechet
was an "artist of genius," predicted that this music might be "the
highway the whole world will swing along tomorrow," and even
offered high-flown comparisons to Mozart and Haydn.

Ansermet apparently tried to talk to Bechet to find out more
about the hidden sources of this multifaceted music. What did he
learn? Bechet was the prototype of what would later be called cool.
On the surface, he was genial and conciliatory. He "is very glad one
likes what he does," Ansermet explained, and the conductor noted,
"What a moving thing it is to meet this very black, fat boy." But
when he tried to break through this surface cordiality, Ansermet got
nowhere. He writes, in evident despair, that Bechet "can say nothing
of his art" except that "he follows his 'own way.'"[1]

Just as white writers tried to probe the cool underbelly of jazz,
white jazz musicians were especially interested in cultivating it. The
term *cool jazz* would not become widely used in the jazz world until
the fifties, but when later commentators tried to write its early history, they inevitably traced this music back to the most celebrated
white jazz player of the twenties, cornetist Bix Beiderbecke who,
more than anyone, deserves the title of founding father of cool jazz.
In this fascinating figure from the Jazz Age, we encounter all the
inner contradictions of cool personified.

Someday a great psychologist will write a study of the psyche
of the white jazz musicians from the early and middle decades of
the twentieth century; in many ways they are the forerunners of
the personality type that became dominant among the baby boom
generation in the late sixties. The white jazz player is the outsider
among outsiders, but has voluntarily chosen this double exclusion,
even takes satisfaction in its far remove from social norms and

expectations. He roots for the underdog and the misunderstood, and he often sees himself in these terms, even if his own background marks him as a child of privilege. He likes the improvisatory aspects of his chosen art form and brings the same celebration of spontaneity to his life, which is often as experimental as his music. At least it is in his eyes—the more straitlaced would simply see his offstage behavior as wasted and debauched. But for the jazz player, the creative ferment on the bandstand inevitably carries over into day-to-day life, and his ways of dealing with circumstances and situations radiate an artistic quality that persists even amidst dissipation and squalor. He flouts the rules, which he sees as applying to others, not him. He values experiences the way a banker hordes capital. Even if he achieves great success—a rarity, but possible in the case of a few white jazz players such as Stan Getz or Chet Baker or Bill Evans—he still feels like an outcast beyond the scope of mainstream society.

Bix Beiderbecke was the first great white jazz player and the most fascinating case study of them all. During his lifetime, the newspapers almost completely ignored his artistry, but after his untimely death, a host of writers were drawn to his tragic tale. Little wonder it served as inspiration for a successful novel, *Young Man with a Horn* by Dorothy Baker, and later a movie, or that more than a half dozen biographies have been published focused on an artist whose whole recording career spanned a mere six years. He captivates our attention, not just for his artistry, but also because so much in Bix anticipates the future. Too many later jazz players would unconsciously follow the same path, a self-destructive rise and fall, *not* because they had studied Beiderbecke's life and times—far from it—but seemingly due to some inner momentum of the jazz lifestyle and the ways it intersects with surrounding social norms and institutions.

To those who knew him, Beiderbecke was larger than life. Yet so much of his story, as it is commonly told and mythologized, would have been commonplace in the late sixties. A youngster finds himself at odds with the values of his bourgeois family, his rebellion facilitated by their doting indulgence. He has run-ins with school authorities and sometimes with the law. Parents and grown-ups want him to pursue a stable career, but he prefers to find himself, to follow his own muse. He experiments with illegal substances, which eventually prove more harmful than he realizes. He shocks the older generation with his transgression of community mores. He embraces the most raucous and uninhibited music he can find, not just for how it sounds, but also as a symbol of his way of life. How much things change over a half century! Beiderbecke's friends saw him as one of a kind—Benny Goodman wondered which moon he came from,[2] and Jimmy McPartland called him a mystery[3]—but he would have been a familiar type on a 1960s college campus.

Above all, Beiderbecke anticipated the later rise of the cool in the remarkable malleability of his life. As I suggested above, cool became a dominant social paradigm because it was a game everyone in America could play, at least to some degree. Whether they were rich or poor, black or white, young or old, cool offered a path—or at least a few steps—toward the sublime. Who better to prove this than Bix Beiderbecke? He was Everyman, but with a horn in hand.

Born in Davenport, Iowa—the heart of Middle America, only a few hundred miles from the geographical center of the continental United States—on March 10, 1903, Bix faced all the typical constraints that turn-of-the-century America imposed on its youth. He was the grandson of immigrants, surrounded by a social milieu full of middle-class rectitude and striving, but with little opportunity for individuality and self-expression. Grandfather Carl Beiderbecke had abandoned his plans to be a Lutheran minister in West Prussia and instead settled in Davenport, where he married Louisa Piper, another immigrant, newly arrived from Hamburg. Bix's parents, Bismark Herman Beiderbecke and Agatha Hilton, remained in Davenport, as did much of the extended family. Here Bix could easily have lived and died, following in the footsteps of his grandfather the grocer or his father, who dealt in wood and coal.

The young Beiderbecke's personal attributes were modest. His health was poor, his grades were worse, his work ethic almost nonexistent. His looks were anything but glamorous—the inevitable adjective one would apply to his appearance is *baby faced*. His one gift was for music, and he did almost everything possible to squander it. He never learned to read music with any skill or to even play the horn with proper fingerings. He would rather drink than practice. Not much opportunity for fame and fortune seemed in store given these predispositions, which might have predicted a nondescript life of insignificant proportions or out-and-out failure. And to become a legendary jazz musician would seem an impossible dream for this cherubic white boy surrounded by the cornfields of Iowa.

And yet…Beiderbecke broke through every one of these constraints and reinvented his life in stylish, sometimes outrageous ways on the largest stage imaginable. He not only transformed himself, but exerted a magnetic pull on those around him. The significant term that comes up in their accounts is *idol*. Describing his first encounter with Beiderbecke, a moment he calls "one of the great thrills of my life," saxophonist Bud Freeman exults, "Our eyes seemed to meet. Here I was facing this great genius I so idolized."[4] "I worshipped the man," clarinetist Pee Wee Russell proclaimed.[5] And Russell was no wide-eyed fan, but roomed with Beiderbecke, traveled with him, drank and performed with him. "Bix was a boyhood idol of mine," Ralph Berton has offered, "whom I had for one brief spring, summer and fall the privilege of worshipping at point blank range (somewhat to his vexation)."[6]

"Anecdote grew upon Bix like ivy on a wall," Berton continues. "His most ordinary words and acts often took on a fabulous, legendary quality…There was something about Bix that was enigmatic, edged, baffling—that made you want to *do something* about him, you couldn't say exactly what." Berton might have added the word *cool* to the list of adjectives he conjures up for the cornetist, but as we have seen, it didn't have the same meaning back in the Jazz Age as it does today. Yet Beiderbecke, more than anyone of his generation, would define the attitude and lifestyle that would become known as cool.

Various tales culled from the many Beiderbecke left behind define different aspects of the cool ethos in formation. Eddie Condon tells of Beiderbecke making dismissive comments on the need for schooling and education, and Condon responding by trying to point out the cornetist's ignorance: "'By the way,' I said, 'Who is Proust?' He hit a chord, listened to it, and then said, casually, 'A French writer who lived in a cork-lined room. His stuff is no good in translation.' I leaned over the piano. 'How the hell did you find that out?' I demanded. He gave me the seven veils look. 'I get around,' he said."[7] The nonchalance, the conveyed sense that much was going on below the surface under the tip of the oh-so-cool iceberg, Beiderbecke throwing off comments and chord voicings with equal disdain, his ambiguous boast that he *gets around*…We don't even need to be told that the complete English translation of Proust's masterwork *À la recherche du temps perdu* had not even been published in the United States at the time of Beiderbecke's death to appreciate the rich new character type, the cool cat, on display for Condon's edification.

The ultimate test of cool, of course, is the ability to maintain the pose even in the face of physical danger, and Beiderbecke had mastered this even before James Dean was born. Mezz Mezzrow offers an account of Beiderbecke almost being hit by a train while in pursuit of liquor buried near some railroad tracks. With Mezzrow and Russell in pursuit, Beiderbecke takes them on a wild journey through fields, over a barbed-wire fence, and finally to the buried treasure. Mezzrow continues:

> Sure enough, he dug out a jug, handed it to Pee Wee, and started back. But as we were hopping the fence Pee Wee got stuck on the wire and just hung there, squealing for help and hugging the jug for dear life. If he let go of that crock he could have pulled himself loose, but not Pee Wee—what's a guy's hide compared to a gallon of corn? By this time Bix, having staggered down to the railroad tracks, found he had a lot of sand between his toes, so he sat down on the rail and yanked his shoes off to empty them. Just then we saw a fast train coming round the bend. All of us began screaming at Bix to get the hell out of there, but he thought we were just kidding him and he threw stones at us. That train wasn't more than a hundred feet away when he finally woke up to what was happening. Then he just rolled off the track and tumbled down the bank head first, traveling so fast he didn't have time to snatch his shoes off the rail. Those funky Oxfords got clipped in half as neatly as if they'd been chopped with a meat-cleaver. "That just goes to show you," Bix told us, "it's dangerous for a man to take his shoes off. First time I took those things off in weeks and you see what the hell happens. It just ain't safe to undress."[8]

So many stories have gathered around Beiderbecke over the years that they have almost obscured the real story: his music. A cornet solo may seem less cinematic than a looming train accident, but the horn is what allowed Beiderbecke to transform himself from Davenport ne'er-do-well to New York sophisticate. In account after account, those who knew this artist remarked that music was his overriding passion, the magnetic force around which his existence revolved. "Music was the one thing that really brought him to life," Mezzrow would later comment. "Not even whiskey could do it, and he gave it every chance."[9] Wingy Manone makes the same point: "He was always talking music, telling us, 'Let's play this chord,' or 'Let's figure out some three-way harmony for the trumpets after the job tonight.' It seemed to us he didn't want us to enjoy life."[10] How odd that Bix Beiderbecke, the man who destroyed himself through his out-of-control lifestyle and the shaper of the cool attitude in the American psyche, should be recalled by those who knew him best as preventing *others* from having fun…because he was so fixated on his craft. The bad boy of jazz may not have had the patience to study music, he merely obsessed over it.

It is here, in his music, that Beiderbecke's role as progenitor of the cool is most assured. His friend Ralph Berton put it best: "Bix was one of the rarest artists our American culture ever produced: inventor of a new music sound, cool, lonely, inward-looking, as lonely as his own soul must have been in its solitary chamber… born far out of his time."[11] Cool jazz could hardly be said to exist before Beiderbecke. The very phrase might even have seemed an oxymoron to the first generation of jazz fans, akin to "peaceful bare-fisted boxing" or "nonalcoholic moonshine." Jazz was the hottest style of music on the planet, and the great cornetist/trumpeter of the era, Louis Armstrong, was trying to make it even hotter. If you could measure Armstrong's fiery horn lines on the Scoville scale, they would rank somewhere north of the jalapeño and habañero. His solos, rich in syncopation and spiced with high notes and flashy phrases, would exert an influence over all later jazz. Yet this was more than just the personal magnetism of Armstrong's virtuosity—he also seemed to capture the very essence of the jazz art form, which has always tended toward explosiveness, intensity, and high drama.

Compare this with Beiderbecke, whose music was "like a girl saying yes," in the words of Condon. Rex Stewart, who was playing with the celebrated Fletcher Henderson Orchestra when it lost a legendary battle of the bands with Beiderbecke and Jean Goldkette's "Famous Fourteen," later recalled: "You know I worshipped Louis at that time, tried to walk like him, talk like him, even dress like him…Then, all of a sudden comes this white boy from out west, playin' stuff all his own. Didn't sound like Louis or anyone else. But just so pretty. And that tone he got knocked us all out."[12] Again and again, we hear contemporaries of Beiderbecke talk about his tone, the distinctive sound quality he got from his horn.

The poor recording technology of the twenties did not do justice to Beiderbecke's artistry, so dependent as it was on aural nuances. Yet those seeking to understand the cool ethos need to seek out three performances, three short tracks that established the cool as a viable path for a creative mind operating in the midst of the hectic American Century. In "Singin' the Blues" from February 1927 and "I'm Coming Virginia" from May of that same year, Beiderbecke essentially invents the lyrical jazz ballad style, a new approach to improvisation that aims more to move the listener's heart than the dancer's feet. The cornet solo lines bob and weave and float over the rest of the band, which is struggling to move beyond the oompah 2/4 time of traditional jazz and embrace a more modern aesthetic. There is still an edgy jazz quality here, spiced by the syncopations and blues notes of the New Orleans and Chicago traditions, out of which Beiderbecke built his sound. But there is something else, a looser conception, more relaxed and tender, that breaks free of precedents and instead looks toward the future. And not just the future of jazz…the later evolution of popular music would change as a result of this intervention.

Sometimes this transformation would take place in response to an artist's direct contact with Beiderbecke—as one sees, for example in the work of Bing Crosby, who worked alongside Bix in the Paul Whiteman ensemble and adopted many of the cornetist's innovations in his own crafting of a new pop singing style. "The first thing you have to understand about Bing Crosby is that he was the first hip white person born in the United States," Artie Shaw would later explain to Crosby's biographer Gary Giddins; much of this coolness—both in its musical and nonmusical dimensions—resulted from the personal influence of Beiderbecke.[13] In other instances, Beiderbecke would impact the later course of American music through more indirect lines of influence, especially through the work of his frequent collaborator, saxophonist Frankie Trumbauer, who would serve as a role model for Lester Young, the most important cool jazz player of the late thirties and forties.

The third Beiderbecke track that signals his break with the jazz tradition is one on which he, strangely, does not touch his horn. Beiderbecke would leave behind only one piano recording, and even that single testament of his keyboard work would never have come to us if his friend and bandmate Trumbauer had not prodded him to give it a try during a September 1927 session in New York. Even today, jazz critics still argue about "In a Mist," as this song was named. Some refuse to accept that this peculiar track has anything to do with jazz. Others hail it as a visionary musical landscape, a snapshot of a future jazz that might have been, if only…If only Beiderbecke had lived longer, if only he had applied himself to formal musical studies, if only other players had been advanced enough to follow up on his leads. But none of these might-have-beens came to pass. As a result, "In a Mist" is a one-of-a-kind performance, unlike any other jazz composition of its era.

Yet if we fast-forward several decades, we can see that Beiderbecke was exploring the same pathways that the cool jazz musicians of the fifties would later travel. Here are the same impressionist harmonies, reminiscent of Debussy's and Ravel's classical music, that jazz pianists and composers would adopt during the close of the Eisenhower years. Here is the attenuated sense of rhythm, more floating than driving, and with a less overt use of syncopation, that reminds us of so many jazz performances from the second half of the twentieth century. While other jazz keyboardists of the twenties hold on to the heavy stride beat they inherited from ragtime, Beiderbecke hears another way of integrating the left and right hands. Here he crafts a unique sound that has freed itself from cliché, from the expectations of dancers, from the heavy anchor of the ground rhythm. The mood captures perfectly the paradox of cool, offering both an emotional immediacy as well as an impenetrable aloofness—a formula that defies precise formulation yet is so pervasive in later pop culture. The music invites us into the composer's inner sanctum, yet vigilantly defends a psychological border beyond which the listener is not allowed to pass. "In a Mist"—the title is apt. For instead of the clang and clash of typical 1920s jazz, we have something less clearly defined, seen through a glass darkly, yet cool and brisk, invigorating in its willingness to go against the crowd.

This should have been the start of Beiderbecke's great years. And, for the briefest of spells, it seemed as if his moment had arrived. A few weeks after this recording, the cornetist was invited to join the Paul Whiteman Orchestra, the most popular commercial band of its day (that year alone, Whiteman had eighteen hit recordings). Yet this ensemble was not a full-fledged jazz outfit, and much of its reputation was built on intricate charts that flummoxed Beiderbecke, who was still a poor reader of music. The financial aspects of this relationship were no doubt more to his liking: Beiderbecke was now paid $200 per week. This might have been the middle of the band's pay scale, but a sizable salary at a time when the average American family made $1,300 per year. Even so, too much of Beiderbecke's earnings went to support his drinking habit.

Before the close of 1928, Beiderbecke found himself a patient at River Crest Sanitarium. He had passed out during a concert in Cleveland and was in such bad physical condition that he was unable to leave town with the Whiteman band. When Beiderbecke returned to New York, the bandleader insisted that his star soloist receive medical care and even arranged for his hospitalization. Beiderbecke may have been just twenty-five years old, but he was already a wreck. He suffered from fatigue, pneumonia, alcoholic polyneuritis, malnutrition, and delirium tremens. Soon after his release, Beiderbecke returned to Davenport for a month of rest and recuperation surrounded by family and friends in his hometown.

Beiderbecke returned to New York in March 1929, but his playing from this point on no longer showed the confident, carefree artistry that had characterized his finest earlier work. Just looking at him, people could tell something was wrong. He had pains in his lower limbs and started walking with a limp. In time, he would use a cane—an ominous sign for a young man in his twenties. He suffered from cramps as well as memory lapses, shortness of breath, shakes, and convulsive movements that disturbed his sleep. He looked pale and was chain-smoking; worst of all, he was drinking excessively again. By September, Beiderbecke was back in Davenport, trying once again to regain his lost health. He was institutionalized at the Keeley Institute in Dwight, Illinois—the Betty Ford clinic of its day—where he remained for five weeks.

While Beiderbecke was undergoing treatment, the rest of the country witnessed the stock market crash, the symbolic starting point of the Great Depression. Beiderbecke, who was in no shape to rejoin Paul Whiteman, saw his own earning power plummet. Even under the best of circumstances, these would be difficult years for jazz artists. But Beiderbecke was now entering his final tailspin, and earning a livelihood required him to leave Davenport behind and return to New York, where all his best intentions were soon overcome by easy access to alcohol. The official cause of his death, on August 6, 1931, was pneumonia. But more than a decade of heavy drinking and a lifestyle out of control were the real culprits. As a result, the father of cool jazz never lived long enough to see how his musical stylings would influence later jazz artists. And, even stranger, how his eccentric, out-of-this-world personality would be echoed in the experimentation and attitudes of the baby boom generation.

The President of Cool: Lester Young

Bix Beiderbecke deeply influenced many of the musicians whose lives he had touched during his all-too-short career. But the most important champion of the cool aesthetic during the thirties and early forties would be a saxophonist who never met Beiderbecke, who instead picked up his influence secondhand—primarily via the recordings of Frankie Trumbauer, who had worked alongside Beiderbecke on his most memorable gigs and recording sessions.

From Bix to Lester to Miles…and from Miles to the wide world outside of jazzdom: this is the main line of our genealogy of the cool. Lester Young would be the leading champion of cool during an age that did not yet recognize its power. Young not only defined the cool sound during these years, but by many accounts was responsible for the word *cool* taking on its new meaning of "hipness." And like Beiderbecke, Young was just as influential in establishing cool as a way of life, a type of style, and attitude that stood out from the crowd.

Years ago, I got into a heated discussion with a musician who insisted that Lester Young had exerted more influence on music than any other jazz player. "How can you justify that?" I asked. "What about Louis Armstrong or Duke Ellington or John Coltrane or Charlie Parker? How can you rate Young above them and all the other great jazz artists?" His response was fascinating and difficult to refute: "Louis or Duke might have had more influence *within* the world of jazz. But Lester was the cat whose influence went outside jazz, into the mainstream of popular music." His cool sound was the jazz style that everybody could learn from—Hollywood composers, bossa nova artists, pop singers, commercial arrangers. You didn't need to be a jazz musician to borrow from Lester. His melodic approach was adaptable to almost every other style. In short, the vision of jazz that entered the mainstream of American life was not the New Orleans stylings of Satchmo or the modal explorations of Coltrane or the so-called jungle sound of Ellington. It was Lester Young's cool jazz.

My friend was talking primarily about Lester Young as a musician. Yet, curiously enough, the same point could be made about Young the person. Young's odd ways of talking and acting and the hipper-than-thou demeanor of his offstage persona would come to be borrowed more often, imitated more widely, than even his saxophone phrases. In truth, everything about Lester Young was striking, from his attire—ankle-length coats, porkpie hats, tab collars, pointed shoes with Cuban heels, pinstriped suits—to his odd mannerisms. "If he was upset, he'd take a small whisk broom he kept in his top jacket pocket," pianist Jimmy Rowles explains, "and sweep off his left shoulder." Rowles continues, "Of all the people I've met in this business, Lester was unique," but he quickly adds, "he was alone."[1] Musician John Lewis elaborates: "He was a living, walking poet. He was so quiet that when he talked each sentence came out like a little explosion."

Here are some of the choicer phrases that were part of Young's private language. A few of them have been adopted by others, but when Young was using them, he was a lexicographer unto himself.[2]

Bing Crosby (or sometimes Bob Crosby): A police officer

bread: Money. When asking how much a job paid, Young would ask, "How does the bread smell?"

bruised: To fail at something

crib: (1) One's home; (2) a musician's style or bag of tricks

deep-sea diver: A bass player, especially one who played a low note that Young liked

gray boy: A white man

Johnny Deathbed: An ill person

needle dancer: A heroin user

way-back: A woman known from some time before

Young also gave many of the musicians he played with lasting nick-names—for example, Billie Holiday, who still is known as Lady Day, the title given to her by Young. Holiday returned the favor, calling

the saxophonist Prez—short for president—a nickname that has
also kept its currency.

Although he was one of the quietest people in the jazz world,
Young was never at a loss for words when a sly rejoinder was
needed. When a sideman complained about how little Young paid
the musicians in his band, he announced, "You have to save your
pennies if you want to play with Prez." His odd jargon often amused
people, but Young also knew how to give a searing, concise critique.
Late in his career, Young was nodding off on a bus full of famous
musicians who were traveling to the next gig. The showy bebop
altoist Sonny Stitt was wandering up and down the aisle, playing
every wild modern jazz lick he could muster. When he got to Prez,
he was showing off all his fanciest phrases and taunted the older
musician: "Hey, Prez, whadda you think of that?" Young looked up
and simply said, "Yes, Lady Stitt, but can you sing me a song?"[3]

Certainly, what Young could do better than anyone was sing
a song on the sax, celebrate the melodic essence of the music, and
find a heartfelt strain that was often lost in the jazz stylings of other
horn players. People who visited him were often surprised to find
that Young didn't listen to many instrumental jazz recordings, but
preferred singers such as Frank Sinatra or Billie Holiday. He often
said that musicians needed to know the *words* to the songs before
they tried to play them. When Young played his horn, one heard
this commitment to the emotional core of the music.

When Young started out, Coleman Hawkins was the acknowledged father of the tenor sax, and most players emulated Hawk's
extroverted, muscular approach rather than the cooler sounds of
Beiderbecke's colleague Frankie Trumbauer. But Young idolized
Trumbauer—we even hear of him carrying a copy of Trumbauer
and Beiderbecke's recording of "Singin' the Blues" in his sax case—
and as a result developed a sound that was lighter, a tone that was
more feminine, than his contemporaries. His horn lines were lithe
and elusive, more willing to linger on notes outside the chords; his
phrases tended to float over the band rather than drive it. When
Young replaced Hawkins in the Fletcher Henderson band, the move
highlighted the sharp contrast in these two opposed schools of sax-
ophony. The bandleader's wife, Leora Henderson, was so unhappy
with the change that she would wake up Young early each morning
and force him to listen to Hawkins's records—in the hope that some
of the older player's sound would rub off on Lester.

Young refused to budge in how he played the horn. His style,
which had first seemed strange and outside the accepted jazz
vocabulary, would come to change everything it touched. Through

his work with the Count Basie band, Young would eventually gain renown as one of the leading soloists of his generation. In the years following World War II, Young's influence expanded further. Charlie Parker, the leading saxophonist of the younger generation, learned his craft by studying Lester Young records, and as the decade drew to a close, a host of young horn players—Stan Getz, Zoot Sims, Al Cohn, Gerry Mulligan, and others—would embrace Young's example, thus anticipating the rise of cool jazz right around the corner. One Prez follower, tenorist Brew Moore, was so captivated by his idol that he announced, in a much quoted aphorism: "Anybody who doesn't play like Prez is wrong!"

Although Young's many recordings as a leader serve as a telling reminder of his artistry, his greatest moments seemed to come about when, in true cool form, he stepped into the background and worked in a supporting role behind a singer, as on his great collaborations with jazz singer Billie Holiday. The partnership between these two artists stands out as perhaps the most inspired collaboration in the history of jazz. Holiday was developing a more emotionally supple style of singing, rich in psychological implication and deep in its pathos. The improvements in amplification and microphones of the era had allowed for a more nuanced approach, and Holiday's own genius, married to her troubled personal history, helped her forge a whole new sense of what jazz and popular music singing might be. More than anyone else, Young understood this aesthetic vision, and his presence on a series of recordings with Holiday had a transfiguring impact on the proceedings. His horn lines help establish the intimate atmosphere and probe the depths of the music—achievements all the more remarkable when one considers the poor Tin Pan Alley material Holiday was often given by her producers and, even more striking, how little Young actually plays on these tracks. Sometimes he is given a brief solo of just a few seconds, or he simply plays obbligato lines behind Holiday's vocals. But his impact on the overall sound is out of proportion to the number of notes he contributes. This, too, was part of the emerging cool ethos, which developed a less-is-more philosophy—an approach that no musician in the late 1930s or early 1940s understood better than Lester Young.

More to the point for our study, Young was widely believed by those who knew him to be the person who developed the modern meaning of the word *cool*. You won't see him cited in your dictionary, but his bandmates looked to him as the first person to use *cool* in its modern sense of "a fashionable hipness." Phil Schaap, who knew many of the musicians who worked with Young, in the Basie

band and other settings, provides this impressive list of jazz artists
who believed Prez coined this usage: Buck Clayton, Eddie Durham,
Harry "Sweets" Edison, Freddie Green, Helen Humes, Jo Jones, Ed
Lewis, Dan Minor, Benny Morton, Buddy Tate, Earle Warren, Dicky
Wells, Jay McShann, and Gene Ramey.[4] These were cool cats in
their own right, and their validation of Young's importance in this
regard is more eloquent testimony than anything found in Funk &
Wagnalls.

Thus with Young, as with Beiderbecke (and, as we will soon see,
again with Miles Davis), we have that rare conjunction in which
the master of cool music is also the revolutionary architect of a cool
persona. In short, Lester Young did not need to have a saxophone
in his hand in order to influence the broader American culture. By
sheer force of personality and creative license in leading his day-to-
day life, Prez set an example that millions would later follow.

We should take a moment to ponder the strangeness of this
turn of events. Of all the figures in American public life during the
thirties and early forties, Lester Young must have seemed the least
likely to serve as a role model for the future. During his disastrous
stint in the military, Young was diagnosed by psychiatrist Lawrence
Radice as "a constitutional psychopath." Neuropsychologist Luis
Perelman supported these findings and added charges of "drug
addiction (marijuana, barbiturates), alcoholism and nomadism."[5]
Young's personal style was sometimes so effeminate—an anomaly
in itself, given the macho tendencies of the jazz world—that more
than a few people thought Young was a homosexual. Others
branded him a junkie, a loner, or just a plain oddball. No matter
what angle you take—sociological, psychological, theological,
whatever—Young was a phenomenon unto himself during these
years, a blip outside the normal statistical distribution that indicates
an unpredictable, uncontrollable force. Could this really be the
American who set the tone for the second half of the century?

We need to meet one more patron saint of cool jazz before
we leave behind the smoky nightclubs and recording studios and
plunge into the coolification of American society. And this last cool
musician on our itinerary may be the strangest one of all.

The Prince of Darkness: Miles Davis

Few would dispute Miles Davis's artistry, but his fame is still a bit of a puzzle. No jazz musician has ever shown more scorn for the typical tools of public relations and media management. No artist ever made fewer concessions to the public's demands or worked harder to disrupt the loyalties of the fans he had already attracted. Even in the jazz world—famous for its harsh, macho attitudes and performers with chips on both shoulders—Davis was a breed apart, tougher and more intimidating than all the rest. The coolest of cats had the sharpest of claws.

His unfriendly looks were so famous that when his label eventually released an album called *Miles Smiles*, the very concept amused fans. After all, Davis *never* smiled, and the small glimpse of him on the LP cover with a bemused expression on his face (was that really a smile?) was as piquant as a current-day paparazzi shot of a starlet en déshabillé. He was the musician who pioneered the concept of performing with his back to the audience. He was the bandleader who walked off the stage when his solo was finished. He was the interview subject whose language was so profanity laden that there was hardly any interview left after it was cleaned up for publication. Of course, Davis often saved journalists the trouble by giving them the cold shoulder in the first place. His attitude was so abrasive and his presence so foreboding that he eventually earned the nickname The Prince of Darkness—a shocking sobriquet in an art form famous for giving lighthearted names to its favorite trumpeters (some examples: Dizzy, Satchmo, Fats, Sweets, Hot Lips, Brownie, Bubber, Bunny, Muggsy, Mutt, Punch, Shorty, Wingy, and Ziggy), but a fitting title for this saturnine star of postwar jazz.

The whole Davis persona, a strange phenomenon in the fifties, blends into what we would easily recognize decades later as street-savvy, inner-city cool. But Miles Davis was, in fact, a child of privilege, with advantages and opportunities that few musicians, white or black, could boast. His tough-guy attitude was a later pose, another filter through which audiences struggled to find the "real" Miles Davis.

Born in Alton, Illinois, on May 26, 1926, and raised in East Saint Louis, Miles spent much of his boyhood on his father's two-hundred-acre farm, where he rode horses and enjoyed countrified life. Davis Sr. was a graduate of Northwestern University who made his way in the world as a successful dental surgeon. The trumpeter's uncle Ferdinand had attended Harvard University, and his grandfather, the first Miles Davis (our jazz icon was Miles Dewey Davis III), owned a five-hundred-acre farm and had amassed a considerable amount of wealth at the turn of the century. In this setting, a child who became a jazz musician, even a successful one, was a step down in the world. After Davis had released *Kind of Blue* (which would become the biggest-selling jazz release of all time), *Sketches of Spain*, and those other cool-school hit records, he still had to acknowledge that, for all his fame, he wasn't as financially well-off as his father.

Yet Davis Sr. set the wheels in motion that led to a jazz career for his son, perhaps unwittingly. When the youngster showed an interest in music, Davis's mother wanted to give him a violin, but her husband overruled her. For his thirteenth birthday, Davis received the shiny new trumpet he had coveted. When he went to New York five years later, it was to attend Juilliard, the venerable conservatory that trains the finest classical musicians in the world. But Miles Dewey Davis III had different plans. His passion was for jazz.

When Lester Young visited St. Louis, the young Davis was in attendance and even sat in with the band. "Playing with Prez was something," he later acknowledged. "I learned a lot from the way he played the saxophone. As a matter of fact, I tried to transpose some of his saxophone licks over to my trumpet."[1] Yet the new generation of modern jazz players would have an even greater impact on Davis. A chance to play with Billy Eckstine's band for two weeks put the young trumpeter in the midst of an ensemble that was at the cutting edge of the new bebop movement. Here, alongside alto saxophonist Charlie "Bird" Parker and trumpeter Dizzy Gillespie, Davis got a taste of the experimental currents transforming the jazz world.

"I spent my first week in New York looking for Bird and Dizzy," Davis later explained.[2] Not only did Davis find them, but within a short while he was playing in Parker's band, the most important modern jazz combo of the era. Here he received an education that could be replicated in no classroom at Juilliard—an institution that he soon left behind—as night after night the trumpeter was forced to match wits with the most advanced jazz improviser on the planet. Davis's work alongside Bird was sometimes faltering or tentative, but his progress can be documented on a series of recordings from the postwar period.

Even more interesting, a contradiction was brewing in Davis's musical life. The bebop idiom was hot jazz at its most intense, while Davis's future was in the cooler currents of the jazz world. The trumpeter himself only gradually understood how his personal aesthetic would take him far afield from the musical values of his peers. Davis's meeting with arranger Gil Evans, who had refined a cooler approach to big band music while writing for the Claude Thornhill band, would mark the most important turning point in the trumpeter's career, even more decisive than his apprenticeship with Parker. These two individuals would seem, on the surface, to have little in common. Evans, a white man born in Toronto and raised in Stockton, California, was twelve years older than Davis and had simple, small-town ways that were a world apart from the urban sophistication of Parker and Gillespie. Evans would bring a sack of radishes with him to a nightclub and eat them out of the bag while others smoked and sipped their cocktails. Despite their differences, Evans and Davis quickly bonded and developed a friendship and musical partnership that would last for the remainder of their lives.

Evans's basement apartment soon became a gathering spot for the musicians who would lead the cool jazz revolution of the fifties. These players were developing a range of tools that would change the sound of contemporary music. In their work together, they relied on a rich palette of harmonies, many of them drawn from European impressionist composers. They explored new instrumental textures, preferring to blend the voices of the horns like a choir rather than pit them against each other as the big bands had traditionally done with their thrusting and parrying sections. They brought down the tempos of their music, preferring a slow or medium pulse over the rapid-fire pace that characterized the boppers. Above all, they adopted a more lyrical approach to improvisation—pristine, melodic, and marked by a sensitivity to emotional nuances unprecedented in the jazz world of that era.

After Davis and Evans, Gerry Mulligan stands out as the most important influence among this group. A later star of what would be called the Cool School in jazz, Mulligan contributed more compositions than anyone to Davis's nine-piece Birth of the Cool band, the short-lived group that first brought this new music to the public's attention, and his baritone sax played a key role in shaping the ensemble's distinctive sound. After this group disbanded, Mulligan journeyed to California where, partly due to his intercession, the cool ethos would have even more influence than it did back East. Here Mulligan burst to fame as a leader of what would develop into the West Coast jazz movement.

Pianist John Lewis, who would also achieve acclaim as leader of a great cool ensemble (in his case the Modern Jazz Quartet), was another composer and performer with the Davis nonet. Lewis was an anomaly in jazz: in an art form that emphasized content, he was a pronounced formalist, more fascinated by novel and intricate compositional structures than by the loose and informal blowing sessions that appealed to most of his contemporaries. The same could be said of French-horn player Gunther Schuller, who participated in some of the nonet's music making—Schuller would go on to lead the Third Stream movement, an influential attempt to merge the two earlier "streams" of classical music and jazz into a unique and invigorating hybrid. Altoist Lee Konitz, another participant in the band, came from a different perspective, more focused on improvisation and the possibilities of the soloist's craft. In his work in other settings, especially with his famous collaborators Lennie Tristano and Warne Marsh, Konitz would pioneer a different side of cool jazz, more cerebral and baroque and less heavily arranged than the music he made with Evans and Davis. Yet he, too, would exert considerable influence, and thus demands respect as one of the finest soloists of the era.

Here is the strangest part of the story. For all the talent assembled in its ranks, this historic band was a commercial flop. When Davis's nonet played at the Royal Roost in September 1948, the band wasn't even the lead act—top billing went to Count Basie. Few fans paid much attention to this group, although Walter Rivers of Capitol Records was impressed with what he heard and decided to bring the Davis nonet into the studio for recording. Davis, for his part, found it easier to get gigs playing as a sideman with Charlie Parker, or serving as leader in smaller combos. A nine-piece band simply wasn't a profitable proposition at the time, especially this unconventional unit. Big bands, which had been a hot property a decade before, were now an endangered species. At the close of 1946, no fewer than eight major jazz orchestras disbanded, and as the decade came to a close, few jazz artists had the budget or appetite for risk to start a new one. In this environment, the grand experiment of Davis and Evans soon faded from sight.

But the surviving recordings would exert a dramatic posthumous influence, long after the individual musicians in the Davis nonet had gone their separate ways. These records made little impact at the time of their initial release, but when they were reissued in 1954 with the title *The Birth of the Cool* (a tag that had not appeared until long after the nonet broke up), something magical about the new name—and the music it represented—captured the imagination of the jazz world.

But even before the *Birth of the Cool* title gave this band its marketing clout, musicians were already paying attention to the emerging aesthetic. The sound of the Davis band was echoed in countless other octets, nonets, dectets—formats seldom employed previously in the jazz world, which had tended to build its music for either a larger big band or smaller combo. On the West Coast, in particular, this proved to be an especially popular approach. Here we encounter similar midsized ensembles fronted by Gerry Mulligan, Shorty Rogers, Marty Paich, Bill Perkins, Lennie Niehaus, Dave Pell, and others. Even Dave Brubeck, who would eventually rise to fame on the West Coast as leader of a trio and quartet, first came to the attention of San Francisco jazz fans through his octet, whose formation predated Davis's but reflected this same shift to the cooler end of the musical spectrum.

The cool revolution had an equally profound impact on smaller bands. Mulligan's biggest success in Southern California came in the unlikely setting of a pianoless quartet. Here his aesthetic vision was enhanced by his frontline counterpoint with trumpeter Chet Baker, whose fashion-model good looks would make him into a poster boy for West Coast cool, and the delicate support of drummer Chico Hamilton, one of the most understated percussionists in the history of jazz. A glowing write-up in *Time* magazine helped develop the fledgling band's mystique, and soon crowds were lined up outside The Haig, the bungalow-sized L.A. nightclub that housed the Mulligan quartet, hoping to get a chance to hear this cooler-than-cool ensemble. But the personal chemistry between the members of the band tended more to the hot and contentious, and before long the individual players went their own ways, with Baker, Mulligan, and Hamilton leading successful bands on their own that furthered the aesthetic temperament perfected by the Haig unit.

John Lewis had a much longer-lasting and more stable history with his Modern Jazz Quartet, a group that did more than any other band of the era to explore the chamber music possibilities inherent in a small jazz combo. This group survived, with only one change in personnel, for more than four decades—remarkable longevity in an art form built on one-night stands and pickup bands. The MJQ left behind more than seventy recordings, which encompassed everything from blues to fugues, commedia dell'arte to avant-garde experimentalism. Yet behind the varied settings and song structures, an imposing unity of vision could be felt whenever the Modern Jazz Quartet came to play.

In other words, almost everyone associated with the *Birth of the Cool* recordings went on to serve as a proselytizer for the cool during the fifties. Oddly enough, Davis himself struggled in the aftermath of the breakup of his nonet. This was the low point in Davis's life and career. He fell under the sway of heroin and became one more addict during a decade in which too many jazz artists, including Davis's former mentor, Charlie Parker, were dying from the effects, direct or indirect, of narcotics. "I was in a deep fog, high all the time," Davis would later recall.[3] An article in *Downbeat* on drug problems among jazz musicians cited him as an example, and Davis found it difficult to get work in the aftermath. Capitol was disappointed with the initial sales of the nonet recordings and had no interest in doing more projects with Davis. The trumpeter often took sideman gigs, worked as a music copyist, or even pimped or stole in the never-ending quest to support his habit. He started recording with the Prestige label, and though these efforts fall short of his later classic sessions for Columbia, they show him in the process of paring away at the lingering bebop mannerisms of his forties approach and developing a more personal sound and musical vision. When he kicked his heroin habit in 1954, Davis emerged stronger than ever, playing better than at any previous point in his career. He was ready to make his move.

The breakthrough came about through a chance event. Miles Davis was not initially booked for the 1955 Newport Jazz Festival. He was added to the lineup at the last minute, asked to join an informal onstage jam session for the closing concert. The reasons for this hasty invitation are unclear: it might have been simply due to the absence of any brass instruments in the jam session. Given a feature number, Davis chose to play a moody, slow piece, Thelonious Monk's "'Round Midnight," and his dramatic performance on muted trumpet left the audience spellbound. Davis made light of the accolades he received from this career-changing performance—he just played the same way he always played, the trumpeter demurred. But when the Columbia label, the most powerful record company in the world, came knocking at his door after Newport, Davis seized the opportunity it presented.

The recordings Davis would make over the next several years for his new label continue to stand out today as the defining masterpieces of the cool aesthetic in jazz. The trumpeter recorded "'Round

Midnight" for Columbia and showed jazz fans around the world
what he had demonstrated to the Newport audience, namely that
the young trumpeter who had first made his mark as a fiery bebop-
per had somehow evolved into one of the finest ballad players in the
history of jazz. In other combo sessions, Davis drew on a provocative mix of ingredients, matching his trumpet with the more
aggressive tenor sax playing of John Coltrane and supporting the
horn lines with a relaxed rhythm section that drew on the influence
of pianist Ahmad Jamal. Jamal himself was never a member of the
Davis band, but his light swing and artful use of space fascinated
the trumpeter. Davis borrowed heavily from Jamal's piano trio, not
just in the ambience of his music but even in the choice of songs, as
he crafted his own distinctive sound space.

Davis's growing fame and financial success gave him a platform
to reunite with Gil Evans, whose career had languished following
the *Birth of the Cool* sessions. Evans had found occasional gigs writing for jazz sessions, but more often did pickup work in television
or radio or scoring for singers. Yet he continued his musical studies
and expanded his command of his craft, and when Davis brought
him in as arranger for a high-profile session on his new label, Evans
was more than ready. The resulting 1957 LP, titled *Miles Ahead*,
stands out even today as a landmark of cool jazz.

Many fans may have purchased this mellifluous record seeking
some type of fashionable background music, but behind its relaxed
facade lies a radical reworking of almost every aspect of big band
jazz. Evans drew on instruments that were little known in the jazz
tradition: tuba, French horn, bass clarinet, bass trombone. Davis
switched from his typical trumpet to the mellower flügelhorn. The
ways these instruments blended together departed markedly from
previous big band models, expanding on the vision Evans had
developed with the *Birth of the Cool* band. While larger jazz ensembles traditionally emphasized the contrast or even out-and-out conflict between different sections, Evans worked instead from a more
holistic perspective, crafting grand unified textures where other
arrangers would have featured the give-and-take of discrete parts.
This unifying vision was also reflected in his decision to marry the
individual songs into a type of suite, flowing seamlessly from one
composition to the next, with only Davis as featured soloist. Above
all, one hears the pervasive influence of models from classical
music, especially French composers from the late nineteenth and
early twentieth centuries—unusual sources of inspiration for a
jazz musician at this point in the music's history. In almost every
respect, *Miles Ahead* broke the mold.

Yet the project, for all its unconventionality, proved to be both
an artistic and commercial success, finding an enthusiastic response
from serious jazz fans as well as casual listeners who might only
have two or three jazz albums in their entire collection. As a result,
Evans and Davis were given the green light for follow-up projects:
Porgy and Bess, recorded in 1958, and *Sketches of Spain*, recorded
from 1959 to 1960. These proved just as provocative and popular as
Miles Ahead, and even today all three collaborations rank among
the best-known albums in the history of jazz, continuing to find a
receptive audience among each new generation of fans. By the time
of their 1962–63 work, *Quiet Nights*, the ever-restless Davis was
starting to move away from the laid-back style of his fifties music,
and the trumpeter was unhappy when this record was issued by
Columbia. Although Davis and Evans would occasionally collabo-
rate in later years, their moment of glorious interaction to shape the
cool sensibility was all but over.

Yet Davis's most brilliant work in the cool vein happened without
the participation of Gil Evans. The trumpeter's 1959 project, *Kind of
Blue*, holds an almost unique position in American music, not only
as the epitome of musical cool but, more remarkably, as a symbol of
the jazz art form as a whole. In a hot idiom, this cool classic would
become the most cherished jazz album of all time. Although precise
sales figures have never been issued, many claim that this record has
sold more than any other jazz album. In various polls of favorite jazz
releases, it invariably stands at or near the top. By the same token, the
Davis ensemble that recorded *Kind of Blue* is often lauded as the most
formidable working band in the history of jazz.

Davis had secured the services of tenor legend-in-the-making
John Coltrane even before the trumpeter joined the Columbia
roster. Their relationship was not always a smooth one, often
exacerbated by Coltrane's drug and alcohol addiction (which he
later overcame). For a period, the saxophonist was gone from the
band, gigging instead with pianist Thelonious Monk. But Coltrane
rejoined Davis in early 1958, playing stronger than ever, yet in a
style that contrasted markedly with Davis's restrained lyricism.
Critic Ira Gitler aptly described Coltrane's playing around this
time as "sheets of sound." The speed and intensity of the tenorist's
approach were the antithesis of cool, and much of the fascination of
the Davis band came from the opposed yin and yang forces of the
bandleader and his star sideman.

Into this mix Davis made two additions that set the stage for the
Kind of Blue project. The arrival of pianist Bill Evans (no relation
to Gil Evans), replacing Red Garland in the band in the spring

of 1958, was an especially important move. Evans's understated and introspective keyboard approach would establish much of the mood and tone for *Kind of Blue*, and one suspects that Davis's visionary writing for this album was conceived with this sideman's sound in mind. To some degree, Davis now had an ally in the group, someone who shared his less-is-more sensibility. Even so, Evans was an unusual choice. He was largely unknown in the jazz world—his debut LP as a leader sold only eight hundred copies in the first year after release, despite near-rave reviews in *Downbeat* and *Metronome*. Evans was often shy and awkward, qualities exacerbated by his position as the only white man in the Davis band, and thus the subject of ribbing and an almost fraternity type of hazing. But the contrast was just as striking on the bandstand, where Evans's attitude toward improvisation and comping stood out as a marked departure from the previous and later pianists Davis would hire. Above all, Evans's ethereal method of improvisation had almost nothing in common with Coltrane's too-much-ain't-enough approach. Davis's willingness to put two such opposite forces to work in the same small combo was one of his most daring moves in a career full of bold strokes.

With the rhythm section rounded out by bassist Paul Chambers and drummer Jimmy Cobb, Davis was ready for almost anything. Yet in an uncharacteristic move, he added one more horn to the front line. The choice of alto saxophonist Cannonball Adderley brought another superstar into the band. This young altoist had been a local legend in his native Florida and took New York by storm almost from the moment of his arrival, in 1955. His appearance on the scene coincided with the death of alto legend Charlie Parker, and when Adderley sat in with Oscar Pettiford's band at Café Bohemia, his performance set off rumors of a "new Bird" who was playing a blazing sax. In time, Adderley would be a successful bandleader in his own right, with hit records to his credit, but for two years he graced Miles Davis's band, contributing one more potent solo voice to an ensemble already loaded with talent.

For *Kind of Blue*, Davis presented his band with an unexpected challenge, literally a musical puzzle to solve. His new compositions increasingly dispensed with the typical chord changes that underpinned most jazz performances. Instead, Davis asked his sidemen to improvise using set scales, or modes (hence the term *modal jazz*)—even requiring them to restrict their solos to notes in the prescribed mode. This was not just an unusual request; it represented a renunciation of the whole tendency of modern jazz toward spiraling complexity and all-encompassing inclusiveness.

Even more noticeable to Davis's listeners was the reflective tone and understated mood of the project, which at times approached a pristine delicacy out of character not only with the hot traditions that had dominated jazz, but markedly out of line with the sensibility of intense players such as Coltrane and Adderley. In short, Davis had not only recorded the most celebrated album of his career, but had done so while forcing an A-team of jazz legends to shift gears entirely and develop a new cool-drenched manner of improvising.

One cannot help reflect on the change in reception between this 1959 project and Davis's work ten years earlier with the *Birth of the Cool* band. The latter had passed by largely ignored and unappreciated by the general public, but *Kind of Blue* quickly became—and has remained—a critical and commercial success. Certainly Davis's music had changed during the decade, but the American mass market had changed most of all, embracing the cool with a vengeance. A style of art, even a way of living and a type of personality, the cool had been largely unknown in the forties, but by the close of the Eisenhower years it was poised to dominate all the key cultural spheres in American life.

Of course, an attitude so inherently robust, so versatile, would inevitably become too successful. Cool cats are a bit like bunnies in the outback. In 1859, Thomas Austin released twenty-four wild rabbits on his property in Victoria, Australia, to enliven his hunting. But there were no natural predators for this addition to the local ecology. A decade later, Australian hunters could kill two million rabbits each year without making a noticeable dent in their population. Fast-forward one hundred years, and we can see cool spreading at the same pace through American culture, starting from a small cadre of jazz musicians and spreading exponentially among the millions in the general populace.

And as we will see, a bunny can be held responsible for much of the damage in the United States as well, as cool left the inner sanctum of jazz and took on the mass market.

The Signifying Bunny, or the Birth {and Death} of the Cool for Kids

On July 27, 1940—five months before the first appearance of the slang usage of *cool* in the title of a jazz song—Bugs Bunny emerged for the first time out of a rabbit hole to ask Elmer Fudd, "What's up, Doc?" Here, in the cartoon "A Wild Hare," was the classic encounter between the hipster and the square, a prototype that would become a staple of popular culture fifteen years later. Cool may not have had a name yet, but it had its first media star.

In comparison with this cool cat (okay, not a cat, a rabbit), all the previous animation stars who had dominated the silver screen during the 1930s seemed…well, cartoonish. You could tell just by hearing their names: Daffy, Porky, Goofy, Mickey, Popeye. (By the way, if you jump ahead a half century, you might have guessed that the Age of Cool was coming to an end when these corny names started coming back in style—so much so that the most successful company of the new millennium borrowed its name from cartoon character Barney Google in order to compete with a brand that had adopted the even goofier name of Yahoo.) In the midst of these one-dimensional competitors, Bugs's insouciant attitude found a devoted following, and this indomitable bunny was featured in five more shorts during 1941, supplanting Daffy Duck as Warner Bros.'s most popular animated character. Before the close of the decade, Bugs had been nominated for three Academy Awards and was well on his way to becoming (according to a 2002 poll by *TV Guide*) the greatest cartoon character of all time.

Bugs drew on the prototypes for cool that figured in pre–World War II popular culture. He adopted the irony and sarcasm of Groucho Marx, and even grasped his carrot the way Groucho held his cigar. He borrowed a bit of Humphrey Bogart (who appears in animated form in two Bugs Bunny cartoons). His pose and posture were reportedly based on Clark Gable's in *It Happened One Night*. All this was married to the cynical attitude of the stereotypical New Yorker, a connection amplified by Mel Blanc's voice for his protagonist, which had a dose of Brooklyn and Bronx with a spice of New York Irish.

I doubt that the creative minds at Warner Bros. were familiar with African and African American traditions of the trickster. But spend a few hours watching the old cartoons of this bodacious bunny and you will inevitably be reminded of the trickster-inspired definition of *signifying* we borrowed from Henry Louis Gates and Roger Abrahams back in Chapter Three—namely

> the ability to talk with great innuendo, to carp, cajole, needle, and lie. It can mean in other instances the propensity to talk around a subject, never quite coming to the point. It can mean making fun of a person or situation. Also it can denote speaking with the hands and eyes, and in this respect encompasses a whole complex of expressions and gestures.[1]

Here, in short, was the signifying bunny.

Is it just coincidence that the same children who delighted in Bugs Bunny in the forties became the Beats and bohemians, the advocates of cool and counterculture ways, in the fifties and sixties? Two decades after that remarkable rabbit's rise to the top of the rabbit hole, the leaders of the new tone were all talking and acting like Bugs Bunny. The attitude is unmistakable; only the carrot is missing.

When political leaders change, look at the exit polls for explanations. When technologies shift, ask the scientists how it happened. When the maternity ward at the hospital fills up, find out what was happening nine months earlier. But when the national character morphs into something strange and new, look at how the folks making the change were raised as youngsters. The student unrest and campus rebellions of the sixties can perhaps be traced back to the popularity of Dr. Spock's guide to baby care and child rearing during the postwar baby boom. Similarly, when Henry Ford revolutionized industrial America, he recalled the McGuffey Readers from his childhood (and could quote long passages from them by memory); both the homogeneity of the assembly line and of America's image of itself, despite the reality of the melting pot, were shaped in some degree by these children's primers. Look at the Internet today and see how the entrepreneurs who revolutionized it in the new millennium spent their childhood and adolescence: working the joysticks of their video games. But the first hipsters didn't have Spock or *Pong* imprinting memes on their malleable minds. They had Bugs Bunny.

Over the years, animated cartoon characters have emulated, in various degrees, the characteristics and attitudes of this hipster rabbit. Yet it was not until the cool ethos took off in the late fifties and early sixties that other animators started to understand the commercial value of this formula. Yogi Bear, launched by Hanna-Barbera in 1958, possessed a similar swagger and clearly walked in Bugs's footsteps. Rocky the Flying Squirrel, who arrived on TV sets the following year, brought an unprecedented degree of ironic double meaning to children's television. Top Cat—his friends called him T. C.—earned his animated show with Hanna-Barbera in 1961 and was a genuine cool cat, with a jazzy accompaniment. He even had a gang of buddies who played musical instruments. Felines were now in ascendancy, but none was cooler than the Pink Panther, launched in 1964, who was so low key that he spoke in only two of the 124 animated short films that fueled his popularity, although he took the ultimate cool jazz soundtrack (composed by Henry Mancini) with him wherever he trod. Even today, when "Theme from The Pink Panther" plays at any social gathering, the coolness quotient rises several notches.

But don't underestimate the canine response! That same year, Underdog transferred the complex concept of the antihero, a staple of cool ethos movies, to the world of kids' cartoons. Of course, the supreme antiheroes for youngsters during this whole era, the acknowledged king of cartoons in all forms—books, TV, stage, newspaper—were Charlie Brown and another dog, Snoopy, who, along with their changing cast of *Peanuts* associates, brought a distinctively cool sensibility to all their doings.

One of the key points raised earlier in this book is that the cool ethos in American culture came originally from a small fringe group of jazz musicians whose mannerisms and attitudes eventually filtered into the general public. This was a surprising development by any measure, but it is even more peculiar to see this jazz influence permeate the world of toddlers and adolescents. Nonetheless, jazz music started showing up everywhere in the cartoons of the early sixties. Jazz might have represented only 2 to 3 percent of record sales—and was nonexistent as a music category for children's records—yet almost every animated character needed a jazz theme song. Mancini's soundtrack for *The Pink Panther* won three Grammy Awards and reached the top ten on the *Billboard* charts. Not to be outdone, Hanna-Barbera brought in Marty Paich, a leader

in shaping the cool jazz sound on the West Coast, who started contributing music to the outfit's cartoons. Forget anachronisms, even
Fred Flintstone needed a jazz theme song, despite living millennia
before the invention of the saxophone. His daily commute might
be decidedly prehistoric, powered by his overworked bare feet, but
the music in the background was a classy big band chart based on
"I Got Rhythm" chord changes, a favorite progression of jazz horn
players brought into the Stone Age by Hanna-Barbera musical
director Hoyt Curtin. For *Jonny Quest*, Curtin penned another
swinging chart, again for big band, one that included some of the
most challenging trombone-section writing of the era.

However, *Peanuts* again trumped them all. By the midsixties,
the sound of a jazz-big-band-playing cartoon soundtrack was
widely accepted, even expected. But when Lee Mendelson, producer
of a planned *Peanuts* Christmas special, proposed building his
soundtrack around a piano trio playing very understated cool
jazz, he ran into stiff resistance from CBS. Pianist Vince Guaraldi
was one of the leading exponents of the cool and melody-rich jazz
sound thriving on the West Coast and had even enjoyed a minihit
with his composition "Cast Your Fate to the Wind." But what did he
know about cartoon soundtracks? What did he know about matching music to a story line? What did he know about the musical
tastes of eight-year-olds?

Even Guaraldi's appearance was the kind to give execs the
heebie-jeebies. One day he'd be running around with a shag hairdo
of rock-star proportions, and the next day he'd show up with a
crew cut suitable for the marines, or sideburns and an oversized
moustache, or wearing some peculiar ready-for-the-garage-sale hat.
When you hired Guaraldi, you were never quite sure what you were
getting. His music for Peanuts was true to form—it broke every rule
of the cartoon business. This stuff sounded like what Hugh Hefner
would be playing in the background while shaking martinis in his
bathrobe. Few networks would have accepted this cooler-than-thou
music for an adult drama, but to pair it with a high-profile show
about youngsters for youngsters was to court disaster.

CBS was also unhappy with Mendelson's use of children who
lacked professional acting experience (some of them could not
even read a script) for the voices and had doubts about much of the
story line too. The pacing was too slow, the humor too subtle. A test
viewing for network execs was met with stony silence, although one
of the animators, who had had a bit too much to drink, stood up
and taunted them. "You guys are crazy," he chided. "This is going
to be around for a hundred years." More to the point, Mendelson,

Charles Schulz, and animator Bill Melendez stuck to their guns, and CBS backed down from most of its demands, although the network execs were now fearing a flop of historic proportions.

What happened? Close to half the televisions in the United States were tuned to the broadcast, and the debut of *A Charlie Brown Christmas* would later be ranked as one of the most memorable moments in the medium's history by *TV Guide*. The show would air annually with little loss of popularity. The fortieth anniversary showing on December 6, 2005, won its time slot—although the audience now included many grandchildren of the first audience to view it—and *A Charlie Brown Christmas* is now broadcast on multiple occasions during the holiday season.

Not only did the cool jazz soundtrack contribute to the legendary status of *A Charlie Brown Christmas*, but in some ways it was even more successful than the cartoon. More than four decades after its initial release, the soundtrack still continues to rank among the top ten best-selling holiday CDs when December rolls around—an artifact from the days of the LBJ administration on a list that mostly comprises new offerings from the biggest stars of the modern day. The CD has become a cornerstone in the catalog of Fantasy Records (now part of the Concord Music Group) and is one of the biggest-selling releases in the history of jazz. Guaraldi, for his part, participated on another sixteen Charlie Brown shows before his death, at age forty-seven, in 1976. Other composers were brought in for later Charlie Brown projects, but none proved capable of writing a single theme that came close to the popularity of the original piano trio music.

Peanuts was an important step in the coolization of American kids' culture—and grown-up culture too…but for more than just music. The popularity of the *Peanuts* characters pushed American humor into a markedly cooler direction. The comic strip accelerated the death of the punch line in the world of comedy, a surprising shift away from slapstick and the establishment of more ambiguous, open-ended ways of generating laughter. Sometimes the final frame of a *Peanuts* cartoon would be so understated that an earlier generation would have hardly recognized it as humor. When the first Charlie Brown special was broadcast, the network was unhappy with the lack of a laugh track—that stock signal to audiences at home that it was time to chuckle. But Charles Schulz knew that he was dealing with a subtler type of humor. His best lines were often reflective comments on a situation—what in time would be called "observational humor"—or casual remarks that sound very much like what a precocious child might say in an unguarded moment. Even when a bit of physical humor came to the fore—as when Lucy pulls the football away right before Charlie Brown kicks it, causing him to fall down (a recurring gag)—the joke was never the pratfall, the low-key dialogue that followed it was: "Charlie Brown, your faith in human nature is an inspiration to all young people." "Never listen to a woman's tears, Charlie Brown." "Peculiar thing about this document, Charlie Brown...It was never notarized."

Indeed, the decline of traditional jokes with knock-'em-dead punch lines would eventually cut across all spheres of the entertainment world in the sixties. For its 2005 article "Seriously, the Joke Is Dead," *The New York Times* surveyed a number of humor experts who tried to assess what it was about 1960s America that killed off the old jokes.[2] Some pinpointed the growing threat of nuclear annihilation, political correctness, shorter attention spans, or the feminization of American manners. But it seems that the real explanation is much simpler. The old jokes just weren't cool enough.

The long setup with a big surprise in the final line was too obvious, too staged. And the cool ethos was not about the obvious or the staged. The ideal of cool humor was a bit of sarcastic or ironic repartee that sounds spontaneous, as with Bugs Bunny, or the observational anti–punch lines of *Peanuts*, or—in the most extreme instance—the refusal to say anything at all that distinguished the Pink Panther. The punch line, to the extent that it survived under the new state of affairs, needed to be downsized and streamlined into the now familiar one-liner or serve as a passing moment in a conceptual or observational piece. As we shall see later on, this approach would become pervasive among adults in the late sixties and early seventies, but the children's animated figures were there, for the most part, even sooner. Bugs Bunny was relying on one-liners and ironic commentary while stand-up comedians were still telling jokes about traveling salesmen and in-laws. In short, kids were major catalysts in this cultural shift in funniness—and it was their growing up and becoming adults that helped establish the cool type of humor as the standard for the seventies and eighties. Certainly there had been grown-up comedians who understood the new ethos at a very early stage—figures such as Lenny Bruce and Mort Sahl—but they had been marginalized in the entertainment industry (and, not surprisingly, building their audience in jazz clubs rather than on television); so it was left to the youngsters to bring the cool sensibility into the mainstream of American humor.

This paradigm would remain unchallenged for almost thirty years (although it is now under attack—another sign of the death of the cool). We can look at later successes in television animation such as *The Simpsons* and trace almost every aspect of them to these early cool cartoon protagonists. *The Simpsons* simply took the irony, sarcasm, attitude, double meanings, cultural references, antiheroics, and other ingredients in the formula and raised them by the power of ten. Bart Simpson was Bugs Bunny on steroids, with a dose of human growth hormone thrown in—okay, maybe I can't accuse this diminutive star of HGH, but from a psychological angle, he was involved in a game of one-upmanship with all previous counterculture cartoon characters.

Of course, cool was more than just a code of behavior for television and animation figures. By the late eighties, the cool ethos dominated the mind-set of young Americans. So much so that sociologists James Stanlaw and Alan Peshkin could confidently claim in 1988 that "being cool is not a way of life for teenagers, it is life."[3] In retrospect, this decade stands out as the peak moment for cool, the point at which its influence was unrivaled and uncriticized. The teen-oriented brands that worked hardest to cultivate their cool image—Nike, Gap, and others skilled in manipulating their corporate images—were still in the ascendancy, associated only with glamour and trendiness, all the negative press about third world sweatshops and gang killings over shoes and apparel not yet a blip on the horizon. Many in Hollywood still look back at this decade as the golden age of teen movies; the formula was simple for films such as *Risky Business* or *Ferris Bueller's Day Off*—just take attractive, young stars with plenty of cool attitude, give them the right lines and accessories, and let them break all the school rules. Imagine Bart Simpson, but much, much better looking.

And trends would now move with fluidity from entertainment to real life. If Tom Cruise was wearing Ray-Ban sunglasses in *Risky Business*, you could be sure that this same style would soon start showing up at the malls and main streets of America. And few could imagine Hoover or Roosevelt quoting a teen coming-of-age movie in the State of the Union address, but Ronald Reagan happily borrowed a line from *Back to the Future* in his 1986 speech: "Where we're going, we don't need roads." Then again, the whole idea of having a movie star as president seemed typical of this era, in which people increasingly conceived of their day-to-day lives in terms borrowed from films, television, and music.

But this era and the ethos it represents are now clearly on the wane. Just as the rise of the cool among the younger generation was first signaled by cartoons, its decline can be traced in the same medium. How else to explain the tremendous popularity of Japanese anime and manga and their various offshoots, where the very flatness of characters and encounters, the highly stylized way in which images are rendered, all contribute to the postcool effect. And like so many of the most striking postcool phenomena, the success of anime and manga came by surprise. The American entertainment industry was the last to recognize this trend, which took off as an underground movement, finding its growing market in specialty stores and via word of mouth at colleges and high schools. Parents couldn't understand it. Grown-ups were baffled by its tone and style, so antithetical to the cool ethos of their own youth. Yet its success is another sign of the changes afoot in popular culture.

Today, when I visit my local megachainopolis bookstore, I notice that every book section has been shrinking over the last several years to make room for more greeting cards, knickknacks, DVDs, and the like. All except one. Yes, the section for manga books from Japan (and, increasingly, their US imitators) is getting bigger all the time. Literary fiction is shrinking. Sci-fi and mysteries are getting the squeeze. History is in decline and fall, and I'm not talkin' Gibbon. Self-help needs some help itself, judging by its disappearing shelf space. But these peculiar books, almost quintessentially uncool in their tone, are big business.

It is worth noting that this genre's audience is not just limited to the target market of high schoolers and college students. My youngest son tells me that, in his elementary school classroom, the single biggest cause of fights is Pokémon cards. A day hardly goes by without some significant disruption of school decorum spurred by the popular Japanese franchise. Every generation of youngsters has its own fads and heroes, but this strange Japanese concoction, with its 493 species of fictional characters, is especially difficult for parents to comprehend. For those raised in a climate that venerated coolness above all else, especially in its animated cartoon figures, the simplistic, one-dimensional quality of Pokémon can be baffling. No wonder that the last bastion of cool cartoons, *The Simpsons* and *South Park*, make fun of this Japanese import.

Ever since it took off in the West, naysayers have been predicting the imminent demise of Pokémon. Marketers know that trends and fashions among kids are often the quickest to change, since the core audience quickly matures outside the target age. For this reason, retailers have been reluctant to hold too much Pokémon inventory or devote too much shelf space to a brand that could collapse in a matter of months. Yet this franchise has shown remarkable longevity. The most recent figures show that more than

150 million Pokémon video games have been sold to date, and an especially hot new release can rack up sales of one million in a single week. In 2007, almost ten years after the US introduction, the pace of sales for these games was higher than at any point in the history of Pokémon.

Pokémon will, of course, fade in time. But the postcool attitude shift it represents will be much more long lived. The cultural tone it sets will, to some degree, accompany my children's generation for decades to come. When I was the same age as my youngest son is now, my classmates were focused on The Beatles, not just the music, but also their paraphernalia. My little buddies at our sixties-era kindergarten exchanged Beatles trading cards, even if they had never heard a single recording of the mop-top band—just as the current batch of youngsters is fixated on Pokémon. And it isn't too much of an exaggeration to say that this small detail was a leading cultural indicator of the future evolution of my whole cohort group. Eventually everything from our haircuts to our wry sense of humor would be influenced by the prevailing winds from Liverpool. I recall the old adage (attributed to the Jesuits) "Give me a child at seven, and I will show you the man." I will tweak it only slightly and proclaim: "Give me a child at seven and let me see his trading cards, and I will show you the grown-up."

But the postcool allegiances of the next generation are much more than a matter of cartoons and video games. An attitude adjustment of major proportions is under way and is evident in almost every aspect of the lives of the twenty-and-under generation. I sometimes try to imagine what grief my classmates would have been given back in the day if they had been seen with a book called *The 7 Habits of Highly Effective Teens*. Show up with that paperback at my old school, kid, and you better hope that one of those seven habits is to run faster than the other teens on the block! But this book has sold millions of copies since it was first published more than a decade ago, and even today it consistently ranks among the best-selling nonfiction books for kids. The concept has blossomed into a mini-industry, with workshops, certification programs, and spin-off books. Judging by the sales figures, youngsters are moving to advanced study of the seven habits, purchasing *The 7 Habits of Highly Effective Teens Workbook* or *Daily Reflections for Highly Effective Teens* or *The 6 Most Important Decisions You'll Ever Make: A Guide for Teens* or *The Choice Is Yours: The 7 Habits Activity Guide for Teens*—all by author Sean Covey, a former quarterback at Brigham Young University and the son of Stephen R. Covey, who has spearheaded a similar industry of seven-habit building for the older generation since 1989.

Guides to living of this sort were almost unknown in my generation—unless one includes Abbie Hoffman's *Steal This Book* or Carlos Castaneda's first-person guides to using peyote—but tips for teens now dominate the nonfiction best sellers for this age group. Many of these are spin-offs of similar books for adults. We find offerings such as Jack Canfield's *Chicken Soup for the Teenage Soul* or Joyce Meyer's *Battlefield of the Mind for Teens* or *The O'Reilly Factor for Kids* or *Don't Sweat the Small Stuff for Kids*. Or the knock-offs on the immensely popular "list" concept, such as *The Seven Best Things That Smart Teens Do* by John Friel or *Life Lists for Teens* by Pamela Espeland. Add to this the extraordinary proliferation of books on passing exams—SAT, AP, ACT—and the image one gets of the modern teenager is anything but cool and happening.

But do teenagers really read these books? Is it possible that all these chicken-soup-and-effective-habits guides are given to the youngsters by overzealous parents and then promptly forgotten? Isn't the book dying in the age of text messaging and MySpace? How can a book compete with *Grand Theft Auto* or *Guitar Hero*? Ah, that was the conventional wisdom…until a young wizard named Harry Potter showed how wrong the grown-ups were. Of all the postcool trends of recent years, perhaps none was less expected than this: that the big thing for kids at the start of the new millennium would be to read eight-hundred-page novels. Certainly the publishers didn't anticipate this. Author J. K. Rowling spent a year trying to find a home for her first Harry Potter book. It was rejected time and time again. She heard repeatedly that books set in school don't appeal to youngsters, who are "too cool" for that type of tale. And her unconventional hero, an unassuming boy who wears glasses and whose most distinguishing personal feature is a disfiguring scar, is anything but larger-than-life. Despite his magical powers, Potter stands out for his very Everyman-ish (Everyboy-ish?) qualities.

Once again, I can't help comparing Pottermania to my own youth and to the heroes who captivated my generation when we were between the ages of five and fifteen. For me and the boys I knew, spies, superheroes, and astronauts were the rage. The success-ful James Bond franchise spawned more than a half dozen popular TV shows during my childhood—*The Man from U.N.C.L.E.*, *I Spy*, *The Avengers*, *Secret Agent*, *The Girl from U.N.C.L.E.*, *Mission: Impossible*, and other stories of debonair and stylish espionage agents who epitomized the cool demeanor in every aspect of their lives, from their wardrobe and repartee to the many very cool gadgets they used in their line of work. The first grown-up book I ever read, when I was in third grade, was Ian Fleming's tawdry

Bond thriller *Live and Let Die*, and I am amazed to this day that
the nuns in my Catholic elementary school didn't confiscate the
paperback when I showed up with it. (As I recall, they did seize my
cousin's copy of *Moonraker*.) But I had an equally vehement passion
for superheroes, who also had their television shows, most notably
the hip and pop culture–oriented *Batman* series, as well as a host of
supporting comic books and paraphernalia. Yet at the very top of
the list, assuming the dominant position in our young male psyches
as the sixties moved toward the seventies, were the astronauts. And
if the real-life ones of the Gemini and Apollo missions weren't dazzling enough, we had fictional ones of *Star Trek* and eventually *Star
Wars* to admire and emulate.

The contrast with Harry Potter couldn't be more profound. No
matter whether you preferred James Bond or John Glenn, Batman
or Captain Kirk, one thing was certain—your favorite hero wasn't
doing homework and being sent to detention by a mean teacher.

I am especially struck by the fact that, for my generation,
almost all of our heroes were grown-ups, while for my sons,
almost all of their heroes, from Narnia to Hogwarts, are kids.
What a contrast! From the era before my childhood, when Zorro
and the Lone Ranger were the rage, through the James Bond and
Captain Kirk popularity of my youth, all the way to Masters of
the Universe and the G.I. Joe redux fad of the eighties, children
wanted protagonists who were bigger and better, cooler and more
powerful than they were. At some point in the late eighties and
early nineties, this started to change. The success of the *Back to the
Future* franchise from 1985 to 1990, with Michael J. Fox in the role
of the main character, can be seen as an anticipation of the Harry
Potter phenomenon. In fact, one could imagine Fox playing the
young wizard if he had been born at a later date. Fox's *Back to the
Future character*, Marty McFly, was a hero strikingly similar to the
average youngster in the audience: one who lived at home with
Mom and Dad, who had to deal with bullies and buddies and all
the day-to-day complexities of life in a small town. By the time we
get to 1990, when the top-grossing film of the year, by far, is *Home
Alone*—spurring another successful film series—we are clearly in
the new era. Protagonists needed to be downsized, and a resemblance to real life—anathema to my generation, but a recurring sign
of the postcool ethos—was now encouraged whenever possible.

Two years more would elapse before MTV stumbled upon
the reality show genre, launching *The Real World* in 1992. But in
retrospect, we can see that the growing taste for "real life" charac-
terizations in motion pictures for youngsters was already pointing

in just this direction. During the planning stages, MTV considered a scripted version of the show in which a diverse group of people between the ages of eighteen and twenty-five (not coincidentally the same range as MTV's target demographic) are forced to live together in a house while cameras film their various activities and interactions round the clock. But the producers wisely decided that unfiltered reality would be more appealing than a polished script. Even so, the end result, as is often the case with the genre, retains a certain overly dramatized quality, leading to accusations of staging and behind-the-scenes manipulation. But give MTV execs their due. They understood the new paradigm before the other networks, and *The Real World* continues to thrive, inspiring a whole range of successful reality offerings for the youth-oriented channel.

Here, in the various pastimes and amusements of the younger generation, we thus see all the key shifts that characterize the move from cool to postcool. Anime, manga, Harry Potter, reality television, *7 Effective Habits*…all of them have renounced the slick and stylized and larger-than-life, hipper-than-thou tone of an earlier day. Instead, they emphasize sincerity, authenticity, earnestness, the down-to-earth—all the dominant elements of the postcool in today's society. It was in these unexpected guises, young wizards and strange trading cards and the like, that the new ethos first proved its power in the marketplace.

What about teen life away from books and TV and other forms of entertainment? Can we see the postcool ethos reflected in how youngsters are behaving in everyday life? Indeed, this is where the biggest changes are taking place! The FrameWorks Institute, in their report *The 21st Century Teen: Public Perception and Teen Reality*, describes a surprising mismatch between the stereotypes of lazy, uninvolved teens and the actual shifts in this demographic. "While adults have serious reservations about American youth," the institute reports, "the reality is that teens place high value on honesty and hard work, and that the vast majority are thinking and planning for their future." FrameWorks shares the results of a Hart Research survey of 1,015 high school students, who in a ranking of values placed "being honest" and "working hard" at the top of the list, outranking other choices such as "having lots of friends" and "being a great athlete." When asked to select the title they would like to see under their senior class photo, 54 percent chose "most likely to succeed."[4]

And many of them are already succeeding. Pollster Mark Penn has identified an important teen subgroup that he calls "high school moguls."[5] He highlights 1.6 million teens who are already making money on the Internet. Forget about newspaper routes and mowing lawns, these kids are going global. No, they won't all be as successful as Mark Zuckerberg, who became the youngest self-made billionaire, at age twenty-three, through the success of his Facebook website. But in ways small and large, the next generation has become very savvy about the Internet's potential for bypassing middlemen and making a small home-based business look much bigger than it really is.

The Chocolate Farm, a Denver-based operation selling hand-made farm-themed sweets, was founded by CEO Elise Macmillan when she was ten years old. She had the help of her thirteen-year-old brother, Evan, who ran the website. By the time Elise entered college, in 2007, her company had ten employees and was getting several thousand visitors every day to its website. AnandTech, a successful technology hardware review site with 130,000 visitors per day, was started by Anand Shimpi when he was fourteen. When Ben Casnocha was that age, he founded Comcate, a company that sells software to local governments to help them track and resolve citizen complaints. Starting at age fourteen, Ashley Qualls of Detroit turned an eight-dollar investment in a domain name into a million dollars by selling graphics and backgrounds for MySpace pages from her website, www.whateverlife.com. Drawing on software he had written during his sophomore year of high school, Andrew Sutherland of Albany, California, launched his Quizlet website in January 2007 and has had great success with this Web-based software for learning vocabulary terms and other information. Some 130,000 site visitors have taken more than twelve million quizzes. Sean Belnick started his flourishing BizChair site, an online vendor of office furniture, in 2001, when he was fourteen, and ran it out of his bedroom. By 2007 (when Belnick was a junior at Emory), the company had seventy-five employees, was headquartered in a 325,000-square-foot facility, and was grossing a staggering $38 million.

Skeptics can carp that these are isolated examples. And, true, not every guy with a beer in his hand at an Emory frat party is running a NASDAQ-sized enterprise in his spare time. But baby boomers, raised in an environment in which all businesses and profit-centered activity were suspect, can hardly imagine how much things have changed. The Collegiate Entrepreneurs' Organization, founded in 1997, now has four hundred chapters and thirty thousand participating students. But there is also the Consortium for Entrepreneurship Education, the Prudential Young Entrepreneurs Program, the Association of Collegiate Entrepreneurs, Future Business Leaders of America, the Global Student Entrepreneur Awards, Mind Petals Young Entrepreneur Network, and even Kidpreneurs, which starts with children as young as age four.

Junior Achievement (JA) is the most venerable of the organizations for young entrepreneurs, having started life at the Eastern States Agricultural and Industrial Exposition in Springfield, Massachusetts, in 1916. But you would never guess that JA is almost a hundred years old, judging by its vitality and growth. In 1959, when cool was entering the DNA of American youngsters, 66,245 students participated in the program, and by the late sixties, annual growth, which had averaged 10 percent during the first forty-five years of JA, had fallen close to zero. On almost any measurement of coolness quotient for teens during the Summer of Love, JA would have been at the bottom of the list. The Ten Days of Resistance, promoted by the activist group Students for a Democratic Society in April 1968, had more participants than almost ten years of JA programs.

Cool almost killed Junior Achievement. As the program continued to stagnate in the seventies, JA commissioned a market research study of 200,000 students and adults, only to learn what was painfully obvious to any observer of contemporary culture. The Johnston Report, which resulted from this effort, noted that "there was negative peer pressure against JA," "there was a lack of publicity, money and facilities," "there was a poor public image of private enterprise," and on and on.[6]

And now? Last year almost nine million students in more than 300,000 classrooms were involved in Junior Achievement. The program is now entrenched in more than a hundred countries around the world. By any measure, it is one of the most popular student activities and has a pervasive impact at elementary, middle, and high schools. What accounts for this remarkable turn of events? Did the people running JA get smarter? Did the organization get some hip marketing guru to redesign its brand and logo? Hardly! The postcool demographic is growing, and JA, which was the epitome of anticool in the sixties and seventies, is now in its sweet spot.

What are these teens thinking? Fortunately, JA sponsors periodic market research to uncover the attitudes of youngsters. What they have learned again runs counter to the general perception of a lazy generation duped by mass media and marketers. When asked to pick their number one role model, teenagers tended to ignore media celebrities and selected either a parent (28 percent) or teacher (11 percent), with the US president coming in a distant third (6 percent). Almost half the students admitted to feeling tremendous pressure to succeed. Yet 87 percent believe they are prepared to enter the workforce, and two-thirds would like to start their own business someday. They are attracted by the potential to make more money as an entrepreneur, but even more by the excitement of having a great idea and seeing it in action.[7]

So the teen millionaire next door may still be an anomaly, but it won't be for lack of trying on the part of the new generation of kids. The new earnestness and postcool attitude is taking root in schools and youth organizations and after-school activities and is setting the stage for what these teenagers will become as adults and leaders. There are many aspects of postcool life that are not quite so encouraging—as we shall see—yet this enormous shift in the psyche of American youth (one largely unnoticed by the media in its quest for the latest bad news) is one of the brighter signs on the horizon.

Let's now turn away from the world of Pokémon and Junior Achievement and look to the world of grown-ups and the larger cultural scene. Here we will find the exact same trends have unfolded, in the same order, but on a much larger scale.

Everybody Acts Like Miles Davis

As the 1950s drifted to a close, *Life* magazine looked back at the rise of the Beat generation and pronounced its verdict on the "Six-Year War against the Squares." The Beats, the popular weekly proclaimed, were the "hairiest, scrawniest and most discontented species of all time." Even worse, "the wide public belief that the Beats are simply dirty people in sandals is only a small if repellent part of the truth."[1]

The danger of this group stemmed not just from its counterculture ways—Paul O'Neil, author of the *Life* exposé, notes that long before Jack Kerouac and Allen Ginsberg arrived on the scene, these same attitudes could be found in Dadaists, nihilists, crackpots, hobos, and whiskey bums—but rather its surprising fashionability. "While most of the forerunners of Beatdom were ignored by the general populace, the Beat generation itself has attracted wide public attention and is exerting astonishing influence." The author proceeds to give an update from the trenches, city by city, almost as if he is reporting on a multifront war or the spread of a new plague.

Here is what he sees happening on the Beat battlefield, circa 1959:

"Bongo drums are beaten at Atlanta's all-night Beat parties."

"The Beats mix socially with Negroes in Washington, DC."

"There are no fewer than 2,000 Beats in Los Angeles, mostly in the crumbling suburb of Venice West."

"There are probably less than a thousand Beats now in San Francisco."

"Perhaps 10 percent of [Beatdom] is Negro."

"Other pockets of Beats are emerging in Athens, Manchester, Prague, even Cleveland and Texas."

The three heroes for the Beat generation, according to this undercover agent for respectability (pause here for dramatic effect): the Negro, the junkie, and the jazz musician. And what were the Beats rebelling against? O'Neil offered a quick and handy list: "Mom, Dad, Politics, Marriage, the Savings Bank, Organized Religion, Literary Elegance, the Ivy League Suit and Higher Education, to say nothing of the Automatic Dishwasher, the Cello-phane-wrapped Soda Cracker, the Split-Level House and the clean, or peace-provoking H bomb." This author doth perhaps protest too much—and over-the-top prose fills up most of the magazine's fif-teen-page spread devoted to this topic. But give O'Neil some credit: he saw more clearly than most folks in 1959 the changes looming in the social landscape and identified their sources in black jazz culture. Perhaps the biggest shortcoming of his diatribe is his naive assumption that he might be able to deflect this social shift through ridicule and ranting.

The Beat movement was mostly a source of amusement for the mainstream media around 1959. A few weeks before the *Life* magazine article was published, CBS debuted its new comedy show *The Many Loves of Dobie Gillis*, with Bob Denver (of future *Gilligan's Island* fame) costarring as Maynard G. Krebs, a parody of the Beat generation layabout. Krebs played bongos, talked in arcane jargon, and routinely praised jazz musicians Thelonious Monk and Dizzy Gillespie (about the only place you would hear those names mentioned on network television). He was laid-back and cool, except when someone mentioned the one word that would set him off...*work.* The previous year, *San Francisco Chronicle* columnist Herb Caen coined the term *beatnik* by adding a Russian suffix to a Kerouacian adjective. Sputnik was in the news, and Caen's coinage made the hipsters seem both up-to-date and distinctly un-American.

MGM released its motion picture *The Beat Generation* around this same time, but just looking at the credits you can see how little the studio took this subject seriously or even understood the new sensibility. Check out the team: Jackie Coogan, a silent film child star who reached his peak of hipness in 1921; screenwriter Richard Matheson of *I Am Legend* and *The Incredible Shrinking Man* fame; Mamie Van Doren, whose imitation of Jayne Mansfield imitating

Marilyn Monroe may have had fans, but not the kind who were reading *On the Road* and listening to Thelonious Monk; B-movie star Steve Cochran, who played boxers and gangsters in many forgettable films and only made his biggest impression on the public's imagination after his death, when he appeared in flagrante delicto in Van Doren's graphic tell-all autobiography, *Playing the Field*. Of course, the producers needed a jazz musician, so they cast Louis Armstrong, who would soon be sixty years old and whose New Orleans style of jazz had nothing to do with the Beat sensibility. A movie like this was just good for a laugh, which was what most of the public wanted out of the Beat generation in 1959. But the laugh was on them. A more probing look at the Beats at the decade's end might have disclosed nothing less than the future of America, bracing winds of change first brought to the public's attention via this group of marginalized, jazz-inspired rebels.

Flash-forward exactly ten years after the publication of O'Neil's beat-up-on-the-Beats article and the release of this execrable movie, and *Life* was now reporting on the Moratorium to End the War in Vietnam demonstration in Washington, DC. A half-million people were gathered for the largest antiwar protest of the decade. And if Paul O'Neil bemoaned in 1959 the existence of one thousand beatniks in San Francisco—the hairiest, least hygienic, and most discontented group in America at the time, as you may recall—let's hope he wasn't walking across the street from the White House on the day of the moratorium demonstration. He would have been begging for the Eisenhower years to come back. By 1969, even Mom and Dad and the Savings Bank had figured out something was afoot.

Let's put this in perspective for a potted history of the cool. In 1949, when the *Birth of the Cool* sessions were taking place under Miles Davis's leadership, cool attitudes were unknown among the general public and were mostly limited to isolated individuals in the jazz community. By the time we get to 1959, when *Life* ran its attack on the Beats, cool had entered the American DNA. Maybe only a small portion of the general populace was really tuned in to its wavelengths, but this group included many of the most influential people in the younger generation. Another ten years elapsed, and adherents to the cool must be counted in the millions. Cool was rapidly losing its counterculture status, becoming the dominant attitude and lifestyle for the under-thirty crowd. By 1979, the whole culture had gone cool. The people who were marching and protesting in the sixties were now consumers, enjoying positions of increasing power. They made tenure or partner at the firm or took over the corner office. As a result, everybody—movie moguls,

marketers, media minions, music makers, moneymen, middle
management, ministers, mavens, and miscellaneous others—had to
adapt to the cool Zeitgeist or else accept a marginalized status in the
new world order.

In truth, the old folks—the parents of the baby boomers—never
really got cool. Yet who really wanted that anyway? Cool would
lose its allure if Mom and Dad were making the scene. Besides, the
old folks never set the tone for shifts of this dimension. When the
big social changes take place, the outmoded ethos disappears not
because the people who follow it change their minds, but because
they simply die out and no one is there to replace them in the ranks.
(The same is happening now with the postcool, which will permeate
society by capturing the youngsters and merely befuddling the
oldsters.)

As we trace this grand history, the 1950s stand out as the key
inflection point, the moment when cool went beyond an attribute
of a few eccentrics and became a social movement. Who were these
five thousand souls, more or less, as identified by *Life* magazine,
who decided to shake things up during the Eisenhower years? What
were they responding to in the contemporary culture that fueled
their rebellion and inspired imitators? And what was it in this
movement that allowed it to conquer, almost effortlessly, the whole
next generation?

The first flickers of the new thing, a movement still without
a name, could be seen in the closing years of the 1940s. *Harper's*
merely called it "The New Cult of Sex and Anarchy" in an article
from April 1947, identifying "a different crowd" marked by "the
stamp of young bohemia," individuals who stand out for their
beards, sandaled feet, and "the barren clutter in the one or two
uncarpeted rooms."[2] In a prescient essay titled "A Portrait of the
Hipster," published in *Partisan Review* in June 1948, Anatole Broyard picked up on this same theme, describing a new personality
type that begins an "inevitable quest for self-definition by sulking in
a kind of inchoate delinquency." In diagnosing this social ailment,
Broyard lists a handful of jazzy terms (solid, gone, a drag, jive)
including the soon-to-be-eponymous *beat*.[3]

Of course, you didn't need to read *Partisan Review* or any other
magazine to tap into these currents, this jargon. Deejay Symphony
Sid's all-night jazz radio broadcasts, listened to by Kerouac and
many of his contemporaries with the fervor of religious acolytes
absorbing holy writ, spread the same message. Sid Torin—sometimes known as "the all-night, all-frantic one"—could even boast a
theme song penned by Lester Young ("Jumpin' with Symphony Sid")

and had picked up on much of Young's hipster talk as well. Sid's bust on a marijuana rap got him fired from WJZ, but run-ins with the law may only have added to his street credibility. Soon Symphony Sid was back in full wattage, first on WBMS in Boston and later on New York–based WEVD—a former socialist station whose call letters came from the initials of Eugene V. Debs. Sid's influence reached far beyond the local airwaves: his ABC broadcasts went out to thirty-eight states, proselytizing for hipness in out-of-the-way locales where no beatniks' sandals had yet trod. Sid even boasted a fan club in British New Guinea, proving that the sun never set on the Beatish empire. This raspy-voiced deejay may only warrant a footnote in the history of jazz music, but his influence looms large in any study of how jazz talk—and walking the jazz walk—made its way into the mainstream of American culture.

For all his passion for the jazz he heard on Symphony Sid's show or in person, Jack Kerouac was far from an expert on the music. Posterity tends to look back at him as the jazziest writer of his era, but his books and magazine pieces are laced with mistakes and factual errors—ones that even jazz newbies would be too smart to make.[4] Kerouac misspelled the names of Charlie Parker, Thelonious Monk, Denzil Best, Bennie Moten, and Billie Holiday. Altoist Hal McKusick becomes, in Kerouac's jumbled head, Al Macusik. He thinks bassist Carson Smith plays guitar, that trumpeter and composer Quincy Jones is a bassist, and that vibraphone legend Lionel Hampton plays sax. Writing in *On the Road* about Red Norvo's famous recording of "Congo Blues"—one of the first great bebop 78s—Kerouac mentions that Max West is playing drums. Who is Max West? Is Kerouac referring to the Boston baseball player? Is he conflating Max Roach and Doc West (two great bop drummers from the era)? But neither of them is on the record, which actually features drummer J. C. Heard.

Yet for all his sloppiness on discographical details, Kerouac responded with fervor to the passion and intensity of the jazz experience and was better than almost anyone at conveying its in-the-moment epiphanies in poetry and prose. His description of Charlie Parker in *The Subterraneans*, his account of a George Shearing performance in *On the Road*, the jazz poetry of his *Mexico City Blues*...these did more than a hundred writers in *Downbeat* and *Metronome* could to establish a new valence for jazz in the public's psyche. Even people who never picked up these books drew on their influence second- or thirdhand. They might not be able to distinguish Dizzy Gillespie from Dizzy Dean, but they knew that jazz and hipness went hand in hand and that some heavy stuff was coming from the jazz scene that threatened to shake up even their pure white-bread world.

This growing influence of the jazz sensibility had little to do with harmony or rhythm or melody or compositional techniques. Kerouac, more than anyone, outlined the *psychology* of jazz. Ever since the decline of the big bands, jazz has barely made a dent in the mass market—today it accounts for around 2 percent of CD sales. But somehow, after it lost its commercial dominance, jazz music gained even greater symbolic importance in the American (and global) collective unconsciousness. Its semiotic richness deepened even as it ceded its preeminence on the hit parade. It became the music of freedom, of release from inhibitions, of the night, of the outsider, of the rebel, of the illicit and experimental. The terms and dimensions of that symbolism (all of them, as we shall later see, eventually co-opted by marketers and pitchmen) were largely sketched out by Kerouac and the other Beat writers during the fifties, and even today their concepts and enthusiasms shape the way in which this music is perceived by the public at large.

Kerouac came up with the influential moniker "the Beat generation" in 1948 in the course of a conversation with John Clellon Holmes, drawing on a word frequently used by Herbert Huncke, a hustler and addict whose dissipated lifestyle made other Beats look like choirboys by comparison. Once again the jazz influence is evident. Huncke associated with musicians, usually the most troubled ones, such as Charlie Parker and Billie Holiday, and even got arrested alongside bop saxophonist Dexter Gordon for breaking into a parked car. But Kerouac put his own personal twist on *beat*. The word that Huncke had used to describe a rough, go-with-the-punches lifestyle, run on the cheap with few chances for betterment, now became for Kerouac a shortened version of *beatific*, a secular holiness permeating the counterculture movement.

But *Beat* was just one of the many names that Kerouac would apply to this emerging worldview, although he invariably returned to this same underlying sense of spirituality. Drawing on Eastern religion, Kerouac also adopted the name *Dharma Bums*, described as a group of rucksack wanderers who opt out of the expectations and values of mainstream America. In Kerouac's 1958 novel *The Dharma Bums*, Japhy Ryder, based on poet Gary Snyder, could very well be looking forward to the Woodstock generation when he shares his vision of:

> thousands or even millions of young Americans wandering around with rucksacks, going up to mountains to pray, making

children laugh and old men glad, making young girls happy, and
old girls happier, all of 'em Zen lunatics who go about writing
poems that happen to appear in their heads for no reason and
also by being kind and also by strange unexpected acts keep
giving vision of external freedom to everybody and to all living
creatures.[5]

The previous year, Kerouac had toyed with still another name for
the movement, the Subterraneans, and here again he made explicit
connections with religion. In the opening of his novel of the same
name, Kerouac announces that the Subterraneans "are hip without
being slick, they are intelligent without being corny, they are intellectual as hell and know all about Pound without being pretentious
or talking too much about it, they are very quiet, they are very
Christlike."[6]

Kerouac rarely gets credit for making Beat into a type of spirituality, transforming it into something more than just "the new cult
of sex and anarchy." Yet this unexpected twist would prove decisive
in the rise of a new cool ethos in contemporary society. Americans
are religious people, so even when they rebel against everything
(including the churches), they want it to come in the wrappings of
transcendental experience. Other Beats had a taste of the beatific—
one summer day in 1948, poet Allen Ginsberg's life was changed by
a divine vision in which poet William Blake spoke to him. At the
dawn of the sixties, Ginsberg would even embark on an extended
spiritual sojourn in India accompanied by fellow Beats Gary Snyder
and Peter Orlovsky. Indeed, to rise in the Beat pantheon almost
required a sense of the mystical, although the sources varied, from
the Edgar Cayce–influenced spirituality of Neal Cassady to the
Buddhism of Gary Snyder. But nobody tapped this spiritualization
of the counterculture more consistently or poetically than Kerouac,
although the particulars of his metaphysics shifted considerably
over the years.

Once again, if we jump ahead to 1969 (the year of Kerouac's
death at age forty-seven), we see how this spiritualized tone permeates the new youth culture, shaping a whole generation's sense
of what is cool and defining the emerging lifestyle—setting it apart
from the typical varieties of licentiousness and rebellion. We find it
in the unconventional opinion leaders of the post-Kerouac generation (who often acknowledged his influence), from The Beatles to
The Doors, Bob Dylan to Simon and Garfunkel, Ken Kesey to Carlos Castaneda. Indeed, almost every aspect of the new movement
would take on a transcendental tone, following the cues set by Ker-

ouac and his confreres: sex moves from the clinical detachment of Kinsey to the higher vibes of Summer of Love ecstasy; narcotics lose their social stigma and are now a pathway to opening the "doors of perception"; ecology morphs from *Silent Spring* alarmism to back-to-nature grooviness; social protest shifts from the strikes and labor conflicts of earlier decades, with their battlefield overtones, to sit-ins and love-ins, everyone mouthing the word *peace*, wearing its now ever-present symbol on shirts and patches, pendants and placards.

This spiritual tinge gave the cool, from the fifties onward, a unique pedigree, made it more than mere fashionability or chic trendiness or self-indulgence. And it is this spirituality that cool has gradually lost. When the concept first captured the public's imagination, cool was a deeply personal aura emanating from a chosen few, more a visionary approach to life than an attribute of consumer products. But as cool became a product-positioning exercise, this spiritual quality was drained from its meaning. Doing a Google news search today for the most recent articles that mention cool, I am nonplussed by what I find. How much spirituality and metaphysics do you get out of these headlines?[7]

"It's Cool to Be Thin If You're a Gadget"

"Cool Vendors Make Marketing Look Hot"

"Ten Cool Gadgets You Can't Get Here…Yet"

"Learning Gets Cool"

"Cool Web 2.0 Apps for Everyone"

"Can Small Towns Be Cool?"

"Top Ten Wicked Cool High Tech Aviation Systems"

The concept of cool is now hollow at the core, drained of the soulful stamp put on it by Kerouac and the Beats. This is why it is so fragile today. If a pollster had asked folks in the late sixties to identify the coolest of the cool, the responses would have been the names of people—Lennon, McCartney, Kerouac, Dylan—at the forefront of the liberating counterculture of the day. Today, the list would be topped by iPhones and iPods and the like. The banalization and commodification of the cool has taken place so gradually, a process unfolding over decades, that it is almost imperceptible until we step back and take a broader view. But you can measure the distance by comparing the coolness of Kerouac to the coolness of, say, the 1993 Gap ad that proclaims, "Kerouac wore khakis." One has substance and suchness, the other is mere gimmickry and manipulation.

Around this same time, Gap also brought James Dean and Miles Davis into their advertising. Smart move? Such appropriation succeeds only to the extent that consumers can't tell the difference between real and ersatz cool. In the case of Gap, they had no trouble making the distinction. Although Gap had been growing earnings more than 40 percent per year when they ran the Kerouac ad, and were generating 30 percent annual store growth, their trendiness was already on the wane, and the following year the execs needed to move downmarket by launching the value-oriented Old Navy brand. And today? "Ask kids what the Gap stands for," comments Eric Beder, retail industry analyst, "and they say it stands for a store they don't go into."[8] Ah, Kerouac still has his edge, forty years after his death. But Gap khakis soon lost the cool quotient they leeched off of him.

The most significant milestone in this process, a half-century-long drama that one might call the Gapification of cool, came almost at the same time that the Beats first appeared on the scene. This turning point arrived when the motion picture industry discovered cool. Hollywood, for better or worse, would develop ways of impacting the broader popular culture to a degree that no writer would ever be able to match. If cool had previously been a matter of personal taste and artistic vision, it now proved that it could be big business, measured in dollars and cents on a corporate income statement. Bix Beiderbecke and Lester Young may have paved the way, Miles Davis and Kerouac may have perfected the concept, but cool would never have reached the highest heights if it hadn't survived the leap to celluloid.

During the fifties, James Dean, Marlon Brando, Steve McQueen, Paul Newman, and other cool icons made their film debuts, and their influence would soon extend far beyond the silver screen. They were defining nothing less than a new attitude, an emerging character type that would shape personalities and behavior styles for the next generation. Of course, the blurring of the boundaries between acting and day-to-day life was a defining quality of the age. The leading lights of the cool persona had advocated it themselves in their championing of Method acting, which was built on channeling their offstage personal psychology and emotions into roles, living the part, so to speak. This approach was no new invention:

it traced its roots back to the "system" that Constantin Stanislavski had formulated during the late nineteenth and early twentieth centuries. But in the fifties, the Method achieved an unprecedented popularity. And if actors now built their roles on blending playacting and real life, who can be surprised if moviegoers returned the favor, emulating the dramatic antiheroes on constant display at their local theaters and drive-ins?

At the same time that jazz musicians were plotting the rise of cool jazz at Gil Evans's apartment on 55th Street in Manhattan, a group of actors were finding inspiration in a Union Methodist church on West 48th, where The Actors Studio first came to life in September 1947, under the direction of three Group Theatre alumni, Elia Kazan, Cheryl Crawford, and Robert Lewis. The studio would move to various locations (settling in its current home on West 44th in 1955) and see many changing faces, but no moment was more decisive than the arrival of Lee Strasberg in 1949. Two years later, Strasberg was heading up the studio and would preside over its successes for more than three decades. Although their backgrounds and art forms were markedly different, Strasberg was not dissimilar to Gil Evans in his ability to draw the best of the younger generation around him and shape their careers with his visionary ideas. Above all, the Method, as it evolved under Strasberg's influence, was a type of stage jazz, emphasizing improvisation, spontaneity, and channeling the experiences of a lifetime into the intensity of a moment put on display for public consumption.

What kind of individual was Lee Strasberg? While Foster Hirsch was researching his history of The Actors Studio, *A Method to Their Madness*, he asked this question of many people. "I was told," he later wrote, "that Lee Strasberg, in addition to being 'like Jesus,' was Buddha, Hitler, Jim Jones, a sectarian, a cult leader, a doctor, a lawyer, a scientist, a guru, a Zen master, Job, a rabbi, a high priest, a saint, a fakir, a badger, a Jewish papa, the Great Sphinx, a Talmudic scholar, a Hassidic scholar, and a human being."[9] This mind-boggling list conveys the intensity of feelings generated by this potent father figure of modern acting—yet perhaps that shouldn't surprise us, since much of Strasberg's Method was focused on stirring intense feelings from those around him. Even more interesting is the odd combination of vague spiritual and secular role models in the various epithets hurled at Strasberg—a paradoxical mixture we identified earlier as a major impetus behind the appeal of the Beats and the emerging cool ethos.

Strasberg was born in 1901 in present-day Ukraine, then part of the Austro-Hungarian empire, but came to the United States as a young child. He learned the Stanislavski system under the tutelage of Ryszard Bolesławski, a defector who stayed behind in the United States after a tour by the Moscow Theater Company. Strasberg developed these ideas through his work with The Group Theatre, which he helped to establish in 1931, but came into his own in the more teaching-oriented Actors Studio. Strasberg would eventually gain renown for his own acting (and even an Academy Award nomination for his role in *The Godfather: Part II*—although he lost out to his student Robert De Niro for the Oscar), but he was initially brought into The Actors Studio because, unlike most of his peers in the field, he valued teaching and mentoring above pursuing his own opportunities as an actor.

America was ready for someone like Lee Strasberg in the fifties. Psychological concepts were becoming legitimized, tempering the long-standing pragmatism of the national character and gradually raising awareness of the complexity of forces driving personality and behavior. This shift in attitude inevitably fed the public's appetite for stage and screen portrayals that probed more deeply into the inner life behind exterior actions. Whatever Strasberg may have intended, his pedagogical system had overtones of the therapeutic, and his encouragement that actors tap into the emotions generated by powerful memories of past events fit in well with a broader cultural context where this same uncovering of psychological depths was seen as a path to mental health and self-actualization. "I would find myself leaving the Studio in a daze," Hirsch writes of his attempts to maintain his objectivity when invited as part of his research to attend sessions usually closed to visitors. "I was beginning to feel that I was becoming the custodian of some special knowledge. Belief in the work is catching, indeed transforming."[10] Can we be surprised then that the actors trained in this Method seemed to resonate in some special way with the general public, crossing the boundary of performer and becoming icons and role models?

No, The Actors Studio did not aim to be a school for cool. But you could be forgiven for thinking that. One need only look at the list of figures who participated, to a greater or lesser extent, in the life of The Actors Studio to see how much this insiders' technique for playing a role shaped the hip sensibility of the baby boomer generation. Here is almost a who's who of cool: James Dean, Marilyn Monroe, Paul Newman, Marlon Brando, Steve McQueen, Robert De Niro, Jack Nicholson, Jane Fonda, Dustin Hoffman, Sidney Poitier, and Montgomery Clift, to name just a few. The graduates of Harvard and Yale might be entrusted with running the country, but Lee Strasberg's students would increasingly be given the job of shaping the American psyche, influencing not just clothes, accessories, and other external trappings of coolness, but also rewriting everything from the speech patterns to the value systems of everyday people.

The jazziness of Strasberg's Method was mostly implicit, a shared sensibility lingering beneath the surface, seen in a new appreciation of improvisation and spontaneity, and the acceptance of the radical notion that the creative impulses of the moment were as valid as more carefully and coldly planned works of art. But there were also more explicit attempts to draw on jazz role models in reinvigorating the actor's craft. Like the Beats, the movie execs were fascinated by the jazz world and sought to tap its power for mass market entertainment. At the same time that Miles Davis was recording his *Birth of the Cool* sides, Warner Bros. was embarking on the first big-budget studio film focused on jazz, *Young Man with a Horn*, released in 1950. Could it be a coincidence that this film was based on the life of Bix Beiderbecke, a father figure behind cool jazz and the emerging postwar lifestyle? Yet the movie (like Beiderbecke himself) was ahead of its time in 1950, when the cool was still in nascent form, and was banned in many countries for its frank depiction of sexual themes.

Even so, the film industry continued to mine the music world for talent that would bring the new ethos to the movie screen. Frank Sinatra, whose film career had floundered in the late forties, found that he was a hot Hollywood property in the fifties—once again, the line between acting and offstage demeanor blurred. In time, directors would learn to cast Sinatra's real-life buddies as costars in Rat Pack productions that not only flourished at the box office, but defined hip bachelor lifestyles for a generation of wide-eyed male moviegoers. Hollywood also tried to make a star out of cool jazz trumpeter Chet Baker, and though he is lackluster in his 1955 debut, in *Hell's Horizon*, the film industry would come back, from time to time, to this troubled yet compelling figure. Baker, for his part, complained what a "drag" it was to get up at six in the morning to make movies, but a few years later he appeared in the Italian film *Urlatori Alla Sbarra*, and at the end of his life, he finally showed up as the lead star in an Oscar-nominated film, albeit a jazz documentary, *Let's Get Lost* (1988), directed by Bruce Weber. As Weber's camera dwells almost obsessively on the old William Claxton photos that make Baker look like the poster boy for fifties-era cool, we get a sense of the ideal type the studios were seeking: sexy, aloof, self-destructive, narcissistic, transgressive, and jazzy.

The studios eventually learned that actors could do a better job of embodying this modern archetype than the musicians themselves. Of course, a real cool jazz icon would be more honest and true to life than a Hollywood construct—but when was coolness ever about true to life? The destiny of cool was to become *larger* than life. There were plenty of hot horn players in the jazz world, but which one could compete with James Dean, brooding and angular and ready to explode? Where was the trumpeter who could make us forget Marlon Brando, muscles rippling under his torn T-shirt as he shouts for his wife, Stella? Could you find a single jazz artist with Steve McQueen's macho swagger or Clint Eastwood's silent intensity or the sensual vulnerability of Montgomery Clift? With Paul Newman's eyes or Jack Nicholson's eyebrows or Al Pacino's hair? Perhaps jazz artists provided the inspiration for cool, amplified by Method techniques, with their jazzy emphasis on improvisation and channeling intensity into the moment, but during the course of the fifties and sixties, the baton was passed from the musicians to the screen stars, who helped disseminate the new ethos to the masses.

Of course, Hollywood already had enjoyed a taste of the cool before the fifties. A new character type had emerged in Hollywood films during the thirties and forties, a contradictory figure who undermined many of the conventions of earlier protagonists. In time, this figure would be known as the antihero—a term that first shows up in the Merriam-Webster dictionary in 1940, a decade before the emergence of cool. Scholars would eventually try to trace this character type back to Old World sources of a distant day, finding antiheroes in the characters of Faust or Don Quixote or Macbeth or some other time-honored figure. But these were mere hints and glimmers compared to the flourishing of troubled and conflicted antihero protagonists in thirties and forties Hollywood films and pulp fiction. The print on the page, the images on the screen may have still been in black and white, but this new character lingered in the gray, indulging in a degree of moral ambivalence and paradoxical behavior that came across as distinctly modern. He adopted poses and exhibited qualities that previously had been more common among the villains of popular tales. Disillusioned, brooding, ironic, self-interested, shrewd, relativistic...qualities that would later reappear in the cool icons of the fifties and sixties were already anticipated, to some degree, by Humphrey Bogart, Clark Gable, and a few other screen stars. Just as Bix and Prez set the stage for Miles, the thirties and forties antiheroes paved the way for the cool actors of the postwar era.

They were lovable rascals, the antiheroes. When the makers of *Gone with the Wind* decided to throw in a dose of swearing—

previously prohibited by the Motion Picture Association's Production Code—to spice up the conclusion of their film epic, they didn't assign the line to a bad guy, but smartly used it to enhance the antihero charm of Clark Gable's Rhett Butler. Its effectiveness can be judged from the fact the phrase ("Frankly, my dear, I don't give a damn") was later selected by The American Film Institute as the most famous bit of movie dialogue in history. With the new antiheroes, their rare moments of vulnerability were hard-won. Gable once claimed that he achieved a facial expression of longing and desire in love scenes by thinking of a big, tender rare steak—a story that reflects the paradoxical combination of hard-edgeness and soft-heartedness that made up the classic antihero. Gable initially balked at the demand that Rhett shed tears after Scarlett O'Hara's miscarriage in *Gone with the Wind*, but finally relented; the resulting scene was one of his finest on-screen moments. Yet Gable ultimately made his mark by disdaining conventions and expectations. Purveyors of Gable lore like to recount how undershirt sales plummeted in the United States after the actor flaunted his bare chest in *It Happened One Night*. Whatever the setting, he set his own rules and followed his own inclinations. No actor of the thirties did a better job of preparing the way for the cool movie idols of the postwar years.

In the forties, Humphrey Bogart took the antihero to the next level. The chronicle of his private life foreshadowed the twists and turns of his public persona. He worked to subvert the promise and polish, as well as the stiffness and formality, of his affluent childhood. In 1918, Bogart was expelled from Phillips Academy, that elite training ground for the ruling class, and never made it (as his parents had hoped) to Yale. Several possible reasons have been given for his dismissal: smoking, drinking, rude language, or perhaps an intemperate outburst—classic Bogart behavior patterns, all of which he would later cultivate in front of the camera while perfecting his persona as the ultimate Hollywood antihero. Bogart had no formal training and never took an acting lesson. All the better—his charm was inseparable from his rawness and the sense Bogart conveyed that little distance separated his on-screen roles from his off-screen personality. When a media frenzy developed in 1950 after Bogart got into a confrontation with some female fans at a New York club, the actor met the press unshaven and in his pajamas. His "explanation"—"I didn't sock anybody; if girls were falling on the floor, I guess it was because they couldn't stand up"—might have been a line from one of his films.

But as with Gable, Bogart knew when to soften his tough-guy image with the right hint of vulnerability—but only a hint. His classic performance in *Casablanca* builds on the conflict between these two extremes, and until the final moments of the film the viewer can imagine his character, Rick Blaine, selfishly stealing Ingrid Berg- man's character away from her husband…and just as easily envision him sacrificing his personal happiness (as he in fact does) for the higher good of the Allied war campaign. This type of multivalent personality—volatile, unpredictable, contradictory—would contrib- ute to the magnetism of cool heroes in the 1950s and later decades. Good guys who were *too* good, in contrast, would soon be losing not only the girl, but (even more tellingly) at the box office as well.

We take such changes for granted these days. Almost every protagonist today, from Bart Simpson to the Terminator, plays off the morally equivocal attitudes refined by Gable, Bogart, and the other antihero stars of the FDR years. But we only need to reflect on the typical entertainment fare of the era that preceded them to understand what a radical paradigm shift this new character type signaled. Heroes had been simple, one-dimensional characters, for the most part, back in the twenties and thirties. The general public first encountered the following protagonists, in print or film, or comic book, during this period: Buck Rogers (1928), Dick Tracy (1931), Flash Gordon (1934), Roy Rogers (first film appearance in 1935), the Green Hornet (1936), Superman (1938), Lassie (1938), Batman (1939), and Captain Marvel (1939). Not much nuance in that list. These were simple upholders of truth, justice, and the American way.

And it wasn't just the movies and serials at the local theater that presented stark and unambiguous contrasts between good and evil. The newsreels did much the same, especially after the outbreak of World War II. It seemed everybody was either a hero or a villain, without much space left in the middle. As they still say in Texas, the only thing sitting in the middle of the road is a yellow stripe and a dead armadillo. When the youngsters who watched Buck Rogers and Flash Gordon in motion picture theaters in the thirties became the soldiers of the forties, none of them wanted to have anything to do with that yellow stripe. Their lives now seemed to be mirroring the stories they had followed as children, enacting large-scale bat- tles fought between forces of light and darkness.

This clarity of roles would not survive the rise of cool. A decade after the end of World War II, the concept of "simple" heroism was under attack everywhere. Bogart and Gable, with their more nuanced antihero complexities, were no longer odd exceptions, but the pro- totype for the new cool protagonists—dashing, devilish fellows you might enjoy on the silver screen, but you wouldn't want them dating your daughter. Yet the public (and, ah, the daughters too) had grown suspicious of innocent heroism, the antinomy of black hats and white hats in the endless cowboy films at the local cinema. They craved protagonists who were edgier and a little out of control.

We can gauge this hunger for a new type of hero by the avidity with which audiences flocked to it when it appeared. James Dean is now held up as an archetypal figure of the fifties cool ethos as it emerged in American films. Yet Dean made only three movies, and only one of them, *East of Eden*, had been released at the time of his death. How could an unknown become a legend on the basis of such a meager output? Yet Dean touched a raw nerve in the American psyche, filling a vacuum that the public hardly knew existed a short while before. This seismic shift can be measured in the surprising flip-flop of gossip columnist extraordinaire Hedda Hopper, who denounced Dean as "another dirty-shirt-tail actor" in 1954 and then gushed over him a year later. "I sat spellbound in the projection room," she wrote. "I couldn't remember ever having seen a young man with so much power, so many facets of expression, so much sheer invention."[11]

A sneak-preview screening of *East of Eden* gave the studio execs a glimpse of the forces they had unleashed. From Dean's first appearance on the screen, the audience began to respond visibly and vocally to his charisma. Youngsters up in the mezzanine, who had never seen this actor before, began to screech and yell in their excitement, and it seemed like the balcony would come down. Writing in *Cahiers du cinéma*, François Truffaut pinpointed the complicated psychological underpinnings of this attraction and comprehended better than anyone that Dean was not just another rising movie star, but the prototype of a new ethos, an emerging personality type. "*East of Eden* is the first film to give us a Baude-lairean hero, fascinated by vice and contrast, loving the family and hating the family at one and the same time…His acting goes against fifty years of filmmaking. Each gesture, each attitude, each mime is a slap in the face of tradition…He belongs to those who pay no heed to rules and laws."[12]

Tickets for the premiere of *East of Eden* at the Astor Theater in New York went for as much as fifty dollars apiece, and Marilyn Monroe showed up to distribute programs. All the stars were out in force…except for Dean himself, who skipped the event. But this actor's absence from the scene only made audiences want to see him all the more, as his death six months later in an automobile accident made eminently clear. Hollywood studios had seen how the untimely deaths of other stars—John Garfield, Carole Lombard, Leslie Howard—had irrevocably diminished the box office draw of their films. Dean, in contrast, seemed apotheosized by his violent passing. He became the first actor to receive an Oscar nomination posthumously, for *East of Eden*, and earned another one for *Giant*. *Rebel Without a Cause* was not only a box office smash, inspiring legions of other "troubled teen" movies, but would become enshrined as a cinema classic, routinely ranking on lists of most popular or influential films. A half century after his death, the James Dean estate was earning five million dollars per year and could boast more than fifty endorsement deals—evidence of both this actor's lasting appeal and the corporatization of the cool ethos he projected.

How do we account for this remarkable success story? Certainly Dean was a fine actor and a dedicated exponent of the Method. Even though his time studying at The Actors Studio was quite brief—although he is often one of the first names mentioned in lists of Strasberg's protégés—he had been exposed to this technique even before coming to New York, through his participation in a study group led by actor James Whitmore in Los Angeles. Yet audiences flocked to Dean's movies not for his craft or mastery of technique. They were attracted to James Dean himself, to the *man* even more than to the actor.

To some degree, this was a result of Method training: Strasberg was obsessed with the ways actors could construct connections between their own lives and individual psychologies and the roles they played. In effect, the exponents of this approach were putting their own personas on the stage and screen, and their magnetism as movie stars had its roots in their characters and psyches. Here we see an accentuation of the traditional contrast between the great British actors—Olivier, Gielgud, Scofield, Caine, Branagh, Connery, Guinness, Hopkins, and the like—who pride themselves on playing *any* role, adapting themselves to its demands, and the classic Hollywood marketing-driven approach that builds from the mystique and offstage charisma of its stars. This had been true before the Method arrived in Hollywood. No one went to a John Wayne movie or a Shirley Temple feature because of the great thespian skills of these performers. They went to see the star, not the role. The same was now true with James Dean and the other exponents of on-screen cool of the fifties and sixties: their popularity was the result of much more than just a better acting technique. Rather, they announced the arrival of a new personality type in American life. No wonder, not long after his death, people even began talking of the "James Dean generation."

Although we tend to see James Dean as an original, a one-of-a-kind movie icon, the journalists and critics who first saw his work invariably compared him to another new star on the scene: Marlon Brando. These two figures were often lumped together, along with other representatives of the new attitude, such as Paul Newman (who had auditioned for the *East of Eden* role that went to Dean). Not everyone welcomed this cultural shift. A critic in the *Daily Mail* called attention to the spread of "Brandoism" as though it were a pestilence and described its pernicious symptoms in clear terms: "The portrayal of a character not recognizably human, by an actor not recognizably acting."[13] Others ridiculed a "mumble-scratch" approach that swallowed words and contorted the actor's body in the name of a faux realism. But just as taunts and insults failed to halt the spread of beatniks and bohemians, the cool in spirit who would come to inherit the earth, the critics' jibes did nothing to diminish the public's hunger for the newest new thing from Hollywood.

Marlon Brando's life reminds us of the same ingredients that had created the progenitor of cool music, Bix Beiderbecke. Brando was born in Omaha—three hundred miles away from Beiderbecke's home in Davenport, Iowa—and fell under the sway of jazz at an early age. The future actor even formed a band, Keg Brando and His Kegliners, in which he played drums. Like Beiderbecke, Brando was drawn by the hustle and bustle of Chicago, moving to nearby Libertyville when his father took a new job. Like Beiderbecke's, Brando's grades suffered and he was constantly running into trouble—making a ruckus in school or spending time in the big city when he should have been in the classroom. After Brando was expelled from Libertyville High, his dad, like the elder Mr. Beiderbecke, decided to send his son to a more disciplined, out-of-state boarding school—in Brando's case, Shattuck Military Academy in Faribault, Minnesota. But this move (again, as with Beiderbecke) only made the son more independent of family influence and midwestern values and did not improve Brando's behavior: he was expelled from Shattuck after being accused of removing the clapper from the main bell. Like the cornetist, Brando furthered his education and developed his reputation in New York and never looked back.

The cool ethos in American life was destined, it seems, to be shaped by bad boys and dropouts. We have a new tone set by Jack Kerouac (dropped out of Columbia), Miles Davis (dropped out of Juilliard), James Dean (dropped out of Santa Monica Junior College), J. D. Salinger (dropped out of NYU), Allen Ginsberg (dropped out of Columbia), Chet Baker (dropped out of El Camino

College)…not to mention the legion of high school dropouts (Marlon Brando, Frank Sinatra, Bix Beiderbecke, Gerry Mulligan, Stan Getz, and others), who never even got enough education to become college dropouts. But if Ivy League degrees were in short supply among this group, the vast majority of these individuals had an arrest, a felony, or even a jail term to their credit. Welcome to the new topsy-turvy world of the cool, where all the traditional measures of suitability and credentialing are turned upside down. Forget the diploma; show us your mug shot!

Like virtually all of the icons of cinematic postwar cool, Brando studied the Method while in New York. Although he spent some time with Lee Strasberg at The Actors Studio, he learned more (by his own admission) from Stella Adler, who taught in the context of a drama workshop at the New School for Social Research. Adler had learned the Method directly from Stanislavski and had later worked alongside Strasberg at The Group Theatre, where the two exponents of the Russian technique had a stormy relationship, driven apart due to their differing approaches to this body of work—Adler emphasizing less affective memory and more the given circumstances. Yet, as with so many of these cult figures from the era, we can debate how much was taught to Brando in workshops versus what he brought to roles from his own persona and instincts. Here is the paradox of Brando saying (of Adler), "Stella taught me everything," and Adler saying (of Brando), "I taught Marlon nothing."[14]

But this was a paradox that was also at the heart of the cool itself, which sometimes could be reduced to a matter of superficial affectations and acquired mannerisms, while at its greatest moments it seemed to rise spontaneously from the artist's inner essence. Yet this ineffable quality also made the cool more fragile than many realized. In truth, this potent personality type and ethos would prove itself to be ultimately unstable and susceptible of collapsing under pressure. By then, the Jack Kerouacs and James Deans would not be around to witness its inevitable decline. Rather it would take a few megasized global corporations to run cool into the ground.

Live by the Swoosh, Die by the Swoosh

In 1984, Michael Jordan had never worn a pair of Nikes. As a rookie in the NBA, he was very close to signing a deal with Adidas, although in college he had consistently worn Converse. Enter Sonny Vaccaro, basketball talent scout for Nike, who asked his bosses how much they had to spend on endorsements. When told that the budget was $500,000, Vaccaro thought it over and proclaimed: "Give it all to the kid."

The kid would soon be called Air Jordan, but the shoes of the same name would become an even bigger business than the on-court activities of the most famous basketball player of all time. In his first contract with the Bulls, Michael Jordan had signed for a reported $3.5 million for five years. But in the first year after launch, Nike sold $130 million worth of Air Jordans, and they continue to be a major Nike line today, long after His Airiness's retirement from the hardwood.

This channeling of fan admiration of a sports star into consumer demand for a shoe represents the symbolic moment when cool became more an attribute of products and less the elusive quality of a person. Other companies had tried to achieve this in the past. After all, that was the corporate dream—put a bar code on cool and sell it at the mall. Have a product so powerful that it was even bigger than the star who endorsed it. Take the élan of James Dean and put it in a pair of khakis (soon Gap would do just this). Take the broad demographic appeal of Tiger Woods and attach it to an automobile (soon General Motors would do just that). Take the counterculture credibility of John Lennon and use it sell to Christmas merchandise (as J. C. Penney would soon do, with a little help from its friend Yoko Ono). But these were just aftershocks in the wake of the tremors Michael Jordan first sent through the world of consumer goods. More than anyone else, Jordan moved cool from the movie screens and sports arenas to the cash register at the big box retailers.

It was only a matter of time before cool found a sports icon to match the allure of musicians and movie idols. The NBA had been founded in 1949, a few weeks before Miles Davis's final *Birth of the Cool* recording session, but it wasn't until the global TV blitz for hoops in the eighties that basketball stars became as well known as entertainment celebrities. Yet when its moment arrived, the NBA was ready to jump ahead of baseball, football, and other sports to set the tone for contemporary cool. As we have seen, the African American community has always served as a leading indicator of cool, and in the eighties, nothing in mainstream American culture captured the mystique of black hipness more stylishly than the world of hoops in general, and Michael Jordan in particular. This was more than a matter of scoring points or even winning championships. Jordan also had the right demeanor and attitude: the low-key shoulder shrug after some gravity-defying move, downplaying the grandiosity even while demonstrating it; the understated comments to the press that buried the boasting and preening in a subtle mist of signifying; the killer instinct on court hidden behind the cool and collected poker face; above all, the sheer style of his spins, swoops, and assorted hardwood hijinks. And it helped that he apprenticed with the master of cool: when Jordan decided to make the move to cinema screens, he chose Bugs Bunny as his costar. Yet the surprise here is not that Jordan showed sports stars could be as cool as film and music icons, but that he could transfer all of this magic to a pair of shoes.

Even in his final year with the Bulls, when Jordan earned a reported $33 million for playing, this was far less than what he brought in from endorsement deals. Which was more impressive, his 32,292 total career points, or his moneymaking arrangements with Nike, Sara Lee, Oakley, MCI/WorldCom, Wheaties, Ball Park Franks, Gatorade, Upper Deck, Bijan Fragrances (for Michael Jordan Cologne), Rayovac, Wilson Sporting Goods, Chicagoland Chevy Dealers, McDonald's, SportsLine USA, Hanes, Fox Home Video, and others? *Forbes* magazine had few doubts when it estimated Jordan's total impact on the US economy at the time of his retirement from the Bulls at a cool $10 billion. For all his illustrious performances on the hardwood, Michael Jordan had become more visible as a shill, as an accessory to various products, as a recurring figure in a bunch of high-priced ad campaigns. In short, Jordan had passed the coolness baton to corporate marketing teams, who could now hatch their various moneymaking schemes under his valuable imprimatur.

Endorsements have been around for a long time—but it took Nike to build them into the foundation for a multibillion-dollar business. Back in 1923, Converse stumbled upon the brilliant idea of putting Chuck Taylor's signature on a shoe and went on to sell more than 750 million pairs of this flagship product. Despite this success, Converse never figured out how the endorsement game was played: they never paid Taylor a commission for the use of his name (although he received a salary from the company, he earned it from his relentless road trips selling the company's product), and when he died in 1969, Converse continued to push its Chuck Taylors to a generation who couldn't care less about the signature from some dead white guy who had played hoops with the Buffalo Germans and Akron Firestones.

By the 1970s, Adidas was already in ascendancy, even in Converse's American home market. This company also had some early history with athlete endorsements. In 1936, Adi Dassler, the man who gave Adidas its name, drove from Bavaria to Berlin to meet with American athlete Jesse Owens and convince him to wear Dassler's special shoes. Owens did just that as part of his historic performance at the Olympics, which resulted in four gold medals. In a significant moment anticipating Jordan's own later endorsement success, Owens became the first prominent black athlete to be linked to a shoe manufacturer. Yet Adidas, just like Converse, never fully bought into the idea that endorsements could serve as the cornerstone for its brand. Like many German companies, Adidas had the old-fashioned idea that product design, engineering, and quality were what really mattered. What a quaint notion, huh? Adidas's logo was a simple three stripes—no signature, no artwork—and the company put its pride and money mostly into technology. By the time of Dassler's death in 1978, his company had accumulated some seven hundred patents and rights to various bits of intellectual property.

This would all change with the impact of Air Jordans. After the domination of Jordan, the battle for shoe consumers no longer took place by meeting the needs of their feet...rather by captivating their hearts and minds. Adidas could stack up patents from Bavaria to the moon and they wouldn't be able to counter the emotional connection that Nike offered with Michael Jordan—along with an impressive supporting cast that included Andre Agassi and Bo Jackson and the Brazil World Cup team, among other megastars of the era. And later would come Tiger Woods and LeBron James and lots of hot prospects hoping to fill their moneymaking shoes as Nike aimed to sign up everyone and anyone who might be a future star.

Let Adidas have its seven hundred patents…Nike would rack up seven hundred endorsements. More than any other company, Nike understood that it wasn't selling products; it was offering a taste of glamour and coolness to the weekend warriors and wannabes and inner-city youths who made up its core market. This hipness comes at a cost: in the pre-Jordan days, a teenager could buy a pair of Keds or PF Flyers for ten dollars a pair, but after Nike changed the rules, having the right shoes was a hundred-dollar proposition. Hey, someone has to foot the bill for the $100-million TV campaign and the fat checks that keep these athletes living in style!

Now jump ahead twenty years. In 2004, General Motors paid Tiger Woods $40 million as part of a five-year deal to promote its Buick line of automobiles. *Buicks*? Don't you need to be sixty years old to drive one of those gas-guzzlers? But, unlike Nike, Buick did reap benefits after it secured a high-priced endorsement by a big-name celebrity. The company faced declining sales and a dying brand during the Tiger Woods era and followed up by suspending its much-needed Zeta project to develop a new generation of rear-wheel-drive cars. Some observers think that General Motors may eventually scrap the entire Buick brand—much as they did with Oldsmobile in 2004. Yet, the problem with the marriage of Tiger Woods and General Motors was less about bad automotive engineering and more about a public that has finally grown cynical of these corporate attempts to commandeer cool celebrities as company shills.

The companies themselves are to blame for this resistance to celebrity endorsements. They created the backlash when they hired Paul McCartney to promote Fidelity financial services, paid Woods (again) to endorse Accenture consulting services, and made all the other inane attempts to buy coolness on the (overpriced) open market. Who didn't laugh when they saw Michael Jordan move from selling shoes to hyping underwear, or touting Rayovac rechargeable batteries? Who didn't grimace when (best of all…or is it *worst* of all) Bob Dole started telling us how to recharge our sex lives with Viagra? And then there were the big blowups, such as Hertz dropping O. J. Simpson as a company spokesperson in 1994 after the former football star was charged with double homicide.

Even within the safe and proven athletic shoe market, high-profile endorsements began to seem less safe as the nineties progressed. Reebok decided they could challenge Nike and built a market share–grabbing campaign around two promising American competitors for the 1992 Olympic decathlon gold medal. Few people had heard of Dan O'Brien and Dave Johnson at the time, but Reebok felt

confident the duo would be hot stars and household names when
the Barcelona Olympics rolled around. The company launched an
expensive eight-month-long campaign built around the good-looking, affable pair. But Dan did so poorly at the US Trials, scoring
an embarrassing zero points in the pole vault, that he didn't even
get an invitation to Barcelona. Dave made it to the Olympics, but
scored a disappointing third. Here was some heavy irony: Czech
Robert Zmĕlik, who won the gold medal, was wearing Reeboks, but
the company had never thought to feature him in an ad.

One might surmise that Nike would be thriving as its rivals
stumbled, but nothing could be further from the truth. The company that had once enjoyed the coolest of images now found itself
in constant damage-control mode. In 1989, sixteen-year-old Johnny
Bates was shot by an older teen who wanted his Nike shoes. One
month later, fifteen-year-old Michael Eugene Thomas was strangled
by a classmate who coveted his Air Jordans. In 1991, Christopher
Demby, fifteen years old, was killed by two youths who lusted after
his ninety-dollar pair of swoosh-imprinted footwear. The media
started highlighting these stories—which had been happening
under the radar for quite some time. When a reporter asked the
Atlanta police department about such incidents, a spokesperson
estimated that they had investigated around fifty sportswear mug-
gings during the previous four months.

But troubles were also brewing for Nike in its own supply
chain. Media outlets were increasingly focusing on the plight of the
workers in Asia who made most of the athletic footwear sold in the
United States. In Indonesia, where many of the Nike shoes were
produced, minimum wage was $1.25 per day—but some of Nike's
contractors balked at paying even this low amount. The inevitable
conflicts this caused would now spill over into the news, as when,
for example, a walkout at the Sung Hwa Dunia factory in West
Java forced intervention by police and military. It didn't take an
economics degree to realize that these workers would need to work
for weeks just to buy a single pair of the shoes they churned out on
their assembly lines. Nor was it hard to figure out which side fans
would root for in a contest that pitted poor laborers against armed
soldiers.

The company that had defined coolness in the eighties was
now a poster child for corporate malfeasance. And this was more
than just a matter of headlines and sound bites. The whole sports
shoe business was in a rough patch. The 19 percent compounded
growth in demand of the late eighties had now sunk into the low
single digits, and the glory days were unlikely to ever return. Nike's

response to all this was…more of the same. The annual tab for endorsements at Nike is now a cool half-billion dollars, and the company's total advertising budget has surpassed $1.5 billion. Yet this endorsement-o-mania begs the real question: If the products are so cool, why does Nike need to hand out so much money to convince professional athletes to wear them?

In all fairness, one can forgive consumers for drawing a connection between an impressive athletic performance and the shoe worn by the competitor. After all, maybe the shoe did make a difference. But what can one say for Nike's next endorsement "innovation"? In 2008, the company announced its plan to brand its Converse line (which Nike acquired in 2003) with insignia linked to famous (mostly) dead rock stars, including Kurt Cobain, the Grateful Dead, The Doors, and The Beatles. Ah, we all know how much John Lennon, Jerry Garcia, Jim Morrison, and Kurt Cobain loved multinational corporations and wanted to help them grow their bottom lines! We know how much these rockers enjoyed wearing Nikes. We know how the choice of a shoe makes a rock song rock all the more…*Not!*

Given these precedents, who can be surprised that the hot brands of the new millennium have increasingly built their reputations on *not* advertising? Google sells around $20 billion in ads per year and has more than one million advertisers, but the company has relied on outstanding performance and word of mouth (word of Net?) for its own growth. Total spending on advertising and promotion at Google is less than 1 percent of sales. Amazon follows a similar strategy. The money that might have gone to fund a big TV campaign is used instead to give breaks on shipping and passing on value to its consumers. Starbucks grew for years with very little advertising, and we have already seen how its decision to ramp up marketing expenditure in late 2007 was followed by a 34 percent drop in the stock price over the next six months—at a time when its competitors Peet's and Green Mountain Coffee Roasters were growing their share price. Few retailers have been more successful in recent years than Costco, but when was the last time you saw a Costco ad on TV? The company estimates that it saves 2 percent per year on costs because of its word-of-mouth approach to brand building. The postcool buzzword in the corporate offices these days is *viral marketing*—but the key to viral marketing is to have the endorsement come from the customer and not some high-paid celebrity. Joe Schmo replaces Michael Jordan…how uncool is that?

Advertising agencies denounce the shortsightedness of this approach. But check this out: ad agencies spend almost no money themselves on advertising. Do they know something they won't tell their clients? Is it possible that a high-priced consumer ad campaign has finally become a sign of corporate failure and mediocrity, rather than (as once was commonly believed) the factor that distinguishes the truly great companies from their plain-Jane competitors? Certainly a growing body of evidence suggests that in the postcool world, more and more savvy brand managers are keeping their logos off the boob tube.

And it is here, on Madison Avenue and Wall Street, that the death of cool will be played out in all its bitter glory. Financial analysts can see a footwear brand like New Balance make its mark as a top-five shoe company and surpass $1.5 billion in revenues… without spending one dollar on athlete endorsements. In this environment, shareholders have started to get nervous about the rapid growth in Nike's future commitments to athletes, a liability that has been growing more than twice as fast as sales. In 2008, the company was forced to disclose, in the small print of its financial reports, that its endorsement and sponsorship obligations surpassed $3 billion—and have tripled since 2002. Clearly here was proof, almost mathematical in its elegance, that the formula that built the Nike empire was on a path of diminishing returns.

But even worse than Nike, more laughable in its efforts to manipulate the cool, is the ever-pathetic Gap store down at the mall. At least the Nike brand (unlike its Converse line) relies on the testimony of living athletes who actually use their products and serve as spokespersons for the company. But Gap's attempts to cool-opt Jack Kerouac, James Dean, Marilyn Monroe, and other deceased icons in its mid-1990s campaign may have been the single most salient sign that the Age of Cool was about to wane. "Kerouac wore khakis"? Maybe he did, but he didn't buy them at Gap. You can *try* to transfer coolness from Miles Davis to a pair of pants sold at a big box retailer, but don't expect people to just nod their heads in agreement. In fact, warning lights should go off. If cool were a stock, you would sell it short when you saw it attached to products at Gap. Even the folks running Gap knew better. It is no coincidence that at the very same time it was pushing these overhyped images of cool dead people, the company was starting to roll out its cheap brand, Old Navy, where jeans were one-third cheaper than at Gap. The first Old Navy store opened in Colma, California, in 1994 (a fitting spot for a corporate resurrection, since this city is best known for its cemeteries, and dead inhabitants outnumber the living by a ratio of a thousand to one), and heavy investment of corporate resources enabled the new low-priced line to reach $1 billion in revenues within three years. In the late nineties, the corporation was opening around a hundred Old Navy stores each year—and the success of this value-oriented chain managed to compensate, in some degree, for the stagnant performance of the flagship Gap brand.

But the new millennium would prove to be unkind for the Gap corporation, with even the Old Navy unit now stumbling. The corporation continued to add stores at a rapid pace, but total net income dropped precipitously in 2000, and same-store sales declined 5 percent. In 2001, Gap posted a $7.7-million loss. Long-term debt had grown to $2 billion. It was losing market share with the over-thirty crowd, and struggling to find younger shoppers to pick up the slack. Media stories focusing on child labor and worker exploitation at factories producing Gap merchandise bedeviled the company, much as they had Nike. Corporate leader Mickey Drexler stepped aside in 2002, but successor Paul Pressler, hired away from Disney, struggled to turn matters around. By 2005, Pressler had stumbled so many times that his nickname on Wall Street was Dead Man Walking. But the celebrities endorsing the products were even deader...the fall 2006 campaign used footage of Audrey Hepburn (1929–1993) to sell black pants—continuing the company tradition of looking six feet under for sex appeal. In short, no resurrection was in sight. Pressler lingered on before resigning in 2007, his reign little better than a disaster-relief effort. Same-store sales were declining again, and the company had become synonymous with cluelessness and a fashion sense so out of touch that even mall rats knew to stay away.

And here was the telling point—not just that a retailer had wounded its reputation or gone out of style. That has happened many times before and will happen again. But the decline of Gap was especially revealing since no corporation had ever tried harder to capture the cool. Every marketing move, every ad campaign aimed to push up the brand's hipness quotient. And this company spent *very* aggressively on ads—more than $100 million on US media alone. Yet the cumulative impact of decades of telling people how cool this company was? A moribund brand with a reputation for terminal stodginess.

One could trace many such examples of corporate cool in decline, but the most important changes are those that cannot be measured at the cash register or by a stock price whizzing across the ticker. The real story here is a gradual transformation in the aspirations and ideals of the general public. As Arnold Mitchell predicted back in the late seventies, an anticool generation has come of age and its values and lifestyles are now driving the macroeconomic changes. The marketing gurus at Gap may think that they are just one clever ad campaign away from recapturing their cool street credibility, but the deeper truth is that they are trying to push consumer hot buttons that just aren't hot anymore.

Researcher Rebecca Huntley has probed deeply into the psyches of the so-called Generation Y, and her findings testify to a backlash against the cool, especially with regard to the corporations that try to co-opt it. "We don't get told what's cool," one young consumer told her. "We make our own choices. We are not dopes. We don't just buy something because we are told to buy it."[1] Only 20 percent among this group tends to shop for particular brands, compared to one-third of the sixty-year-olds. "I don't like people who stick to the same things or are too loyal to a brand," another Generation Yer announced to Huntley. This group, Huntley concludes, is "extremely media-savvy and derisive of those marketers who insult their intelligence with gimmicks and cheap tricks."

Within this cohort there is a subset, small but growing, of ardent resisters. And though the United States is the epicenter of this movement, it is in fact a global trend. Barbara Pocock and Jane Clarke, in their study of young Australians, noted a vocal group who "rejected the pursuit of 'coolness' and belonging through stuff."[2] Professor Vince Mitchell, writing in the United Kingdom, noted a similar group who "show high levels of marketing cynicism, are uninterested in shopping and fashion, and practice forms of marketing resistance."[3] In the United States, pollster John Zogby has been periodically asking consumers over the last decade about the connection between material possessions and the American dream; much to his surprise, his respondents are becoming increasingly nonmaterialistic in their attitudes. "To live in the United States is to be bombarded with advertising messages," Zogby writes. "In theory, we should be obsessed with consumption, with getting and spending." Yet his studies show that "nearly half of those who believe the American dream is attainable in any form in our lifetime now view it in nonmaterial terms."[4]

Perhaps the last holdout for the corporate coolocracy is the third world, where the allure of acquiring status with clothing and accessories, above all with the right logo, is still powerful, and marketing messages are not so cluttered and thus blocked out by consumers. In truth, high-end brands have more clout in Bangalore than in Boston, excite greater fervor in Hong Kong than Houston, draw bigger crowds on Nanjing Road than Rodeo Drive. And even when one encounters cooloholics in major US cities, they are usually the least sophisticated shoppers, especially inner-city youths, inexperienced consumers who are the most susceptible to high-end marketing.

In contrast, the genuinely wealthy have been among the most vehement in rejecting the consumerist ethos. When Thomas J. Stanley and William D. Danko published their research on the spending patterns of the rich in their book *The Millionaire Next Door*, readers were dumbfounded by the findings. Focus groups and surveys found that these wealthy individuals were largely immune to the marketing messages that tried to link status and possessions. These were folks with huge financial resources, yet who preferred to drive a used car, would refuse to pay more than $300 for a suit, would never buy an expensive watch. And these were not just misers or eccentrics. These millionaires were indeed next door, as the title indicated, scattered all over the country, in large cities and small communities, leading their lives unobtrusively and unostentatiously.

But if the wealthiest people in your community are not buying all this high-end stuff, who is? Increasingly, it is the debt-ridden, credit-card-maxed-out people who serve the millionaires—the bank employee who handles their financial transactions or the real estate agent who lists their properties or the maître d' who seats them at the restaurant. Stanley and Danko describe this phenomenon with an old Texas expression: big hat, no cattle. This is a salient characteristic of our postcool society, but one still seldom recognized. As the cool enters its final decline, everything goes topsy-turvy. The people who would once have defined the cool are the most explicit in rejecting its values, while those with the lowest status—the unemployed, servants, gang members, new immigrants, third world workers—remain the most ardent believers. Yet Nike and Gap and other marketers of cool can take little comfort in these last followers of a now discredited creed, since these folks have the least to spend, and their very loyalty will only tarnish brands and accelerate their inevitable decline.

In truth, even in the inner city the dominance of the cool pose is under attack. In 1992, when they published their book, *Cool Pose: The Dilemmas of Black Manhood in America*, Richard Majors and Janet Mancini Billson expressed sentiments that no doubt many in the black community were quietly harboring. "Being cool, or adopting a cool pose as we call it, is a strategy that many black males use in making sense of their everyday lives," the authors note. But at what price? "Coolness as a mask may contribute to dropping out of school, getting into trouble, sliding into drug and alcohol abuse, and being sucked into delinquent or criminal street gangs. Cool pose may be a factor in frustrating love relationships and in violence in the home and on the streets."[5] In short, the quest for coolness may have initially emerged as a survival strategy, but now has brought about unintended consequences that finally outweigh its benefits.

Even more interesting, the two scholars drew many of their conclusions from long discussions with members of the black community, conducted in the early nineties, during which participants would offer up surprising comments: sometimes blanket statements, such as "cool represents something bad," or paradoxical ones, such as "a cool person is a person who's trying to be cool when he's not."[6] The inescapable bottom line was that a reexamination of the cool was taking place within the very African American communities that had nurtured it for decades and bequeathed it to the mainstream culture. Writing in 1997, Donnell Alexander could assert:

> The problem with American culture, the reason why irony's been elevated to raison d'être status and neurosis increasingly gets fetishized, is its twisted approach to cool. Most think cool is something you can put on and take off at will (like a strap-on goatee). They think it's some shit you go shopping for. And that taints cool…Such strains aren't even cool anymore, but an evil ersatz-cool, one that fights real cool at every turn.[7]

This debate would emerge again and again, in various forms and with increasing vehemence, in ensuing years. It took on a bitter culture-wars tone with the arrival of the Ebonics debate of 1996–97. Many linguists had long espoused the view that the speech practices of cultural subgroups are valid languages in their own right. But now this academic perspective became fodder for talk-show hosts and spurred wisecracks from stand-up comedians. Black street talk, which had long defined cool and even inspired so much mainstream phraseology, had somehow lost its charm in short order. Here again we can't help noticing the difference between the early stages of cool's ascendancy, when Cab Calloway's hipster's lexicon delighted readers with its slick talk so representative of the new ethos, and the new Ebonics dictionaries, which showed up on the Web and in e-mails in the late nineties to ridicule black vernacular speech.

Then, of course, came Bill Cosby. His May 2004 speech amplified many of the points that Majors and Billson had raised a dozen years before, but now with an intensity and irritability that made clear a growing fissure within black America itself. The setting was resonant: Cosby was receiving an award on the occasion of the

fiftieth anniversary of the *Brown v. Board of Education* decision. He
spent only a few seconds dwelling on the momentous court decision
before launching into a full frontal attack on inner-city culture.
"Everybody knows it's important to speak English except these
knuckleheads. You can't land a plane with 'why you ain't...' You can't
be a doctor with that kind of crap coming out of your mouth."

Cosby himself was something of an icon of anticool, maintaining his homespun, almost Will Rogers approach to storytelling,
while other black comedians, from Richard Pryor to Chris Rock,
had developed a more up-to-date, street-smart approach. Even as
a young man, Cosby had been old-fashioned in his comedy. Now,
at age sixty-six, he went on the offensive. Perhaps he sensed that
the time was ripe for him to make an outspoken rebuttal. During
this same period, Eddie Murphy was making his transition from an
edgy, Pryoresque comedian to the lovable star of family-oriented
films such as *Dr. Dolittle* and *The Nutty Professor*. Jim Carrey was
the hottest comedian in the country at this moment in American
history, replacing the sarcasm and irony of the seventies and eighties with a simpler, goofier humor that had more in common with
the Keystone Kops than with Lenny Bruce or George Carlin. In an
odd sort of way, this might have been Cosby's moment, the point at
which his personification of the anticool no longer seemed quite so
out of alignment with the American trend-o-meter.

"These people are not funny anymore," he told his audience.
"And that's not my brother. And that's not my sister. They're faking
and they're dragging me way down because the state, the city, and
all these people have to pick up the tab on them...And these people
are not parenting. They're buying things for the kid—five-hun-
dred-dollar sneakers, for what? They won't buy or spend $250 on
Hooked on Phonics." The backlash against Cosby's speech came
from many quarters, and the emerging consensus, at least in the
mainstream media, was that the comedian had gone a bit too far.
Yet when Cosby was actually up at the podium venting his views,
the cheering, laughter, and applause from the audience were overwhelming. Even those who disagreed with his views, or the way in
which he presented them, saw that he was touching a raw nerve.

Many aspects of Cosby's speech went beyond issues of coolness
and encompassed a broader cultural critique. Yet there was a
clear assumption—shared by Cosby and his critics—that these
two matters were closely linked. Cool poses and attitude had, for
better or worse, shaped much of black inner-city culture, and what
one thought of the latter shaped how one perceived the former.
Here was the kicker: even in the heart of the black culture that

had defined cool, a growing number of individuals were seeing it as a cover or a dodge, or linking it, explicitly or implicitly, with shallowness, self-degradation, and irresponsibility. The fact that Cosby specifically attacked exorbitantly priced sports shoes during his remarks was all too revealing. No one in his audience needed an explanation of the connection between the swoosh and the state of inner-city America.

But abandoning the cool is not without its cost. Cool may be corrupted, but it also has its constructive, positive aspects. In particular, this shift away from coolness in the public ethos seems to be contributing to more and more confrontations in public and private spheres and the substitution of shouting and rage for social discourse. Let's now take a look at what happens when a whole society starts to lose its cool.

America Loses
Its Cool

When NBC Radio launched *America's Town Meeting of the Air* in May 1935, little did the network executives realize how this interactive format would evolve. The idea of inviting the audience to ask questions on current events and social issues and broadcasting the informal give-and-take to the nation at large seemed a simple extension of grassroots democracy. But the tone of this early experiment in talk radio is so markedly different from what we hear today on the airwaves that one can hardly imagine how we got from there to here.

George V. Denny Jr., the founder and moderator of the show, may be the father of talk radio, but he was no Rush Limbaugh. In fact, Denny hoped his broadcast would *reduce* the polarization in American political discourse. He forced listeners to consider seriously a *range* of political viewpoints, and even if he allowed pointed questions and a dose of sarcasm, he strictly prohibited insults and name-calling. At the outset of a December 1935 broadcast, Denny shared his guiding principles.

> Let me explain at once that this is not a debate. It is a joint discussion in which two qualified authorities, approaching the problem from two widely different viewpoints, discuss the subject. As we have said before, these meetings are conducted in the interest of the welfare of the whole American people, and in presenting two or more conflicting views at the same time during the same hour, we believe a highly useful and constructive purpose is served.

Such civility would place dead last in the Arbitron Ratings these days. This degradation from town hall meeting to out-of-control melee only took place gradually in the world of talk radio. When broadcaster Long John Nebel instituted the seven-second delay in the fifties, the goal was still to keep the ugliness off of the airwaves. But now in the new millennium, with the rise of shock jocks, "anything goes" satellite radio, and irate talk-show hosts who vie to see who can shout the loudest, civility and decorum are the last things one associates with talk radio.

This is what happens when a whole society loses its cool. The cool ethos, as its very name implied, brought down the temperature in social conflicts, smoothed over antagonisms and disagreements. This was one of the great legacies that cool carried with it from its African American roots. The black culture that created the modern cool sensibility had developed a wide range of attitudes and techniques to deflect conflict and minimize the chances of violent outburst. Perhaps, as Robert Farris Thompson has suggested, these were simply continuations of African techniques of conciliation and gentle persuasion in contrast to the hierarchical and competition-based structures of Europe and the United States. But certainly these methods took on new importance on American soil, where a black underclass daily faced a hostile majority. Sometimes the slightest provocation could result in the most tragic consequences. In this setting, keeping one's cool was not just a stylish way of adding a piquant flavor to day-to-day life. It was also a valuable survival tool.

How does coolness deflect conflict? First and foremost, the cool attitude aims to be above it all, untouched by the surrounding fray. Cool is indirect and oblique and avoids the head-on collision in social spheres. The indirectness is amplified by the frequent use of ironic distance. To stay cool, you must work to keep emotions in check, and when they do appear, they should be presented in stylized, nonconfrontational ways. Cool is permeated with a sense of the comic and is quick to be amused, thus defusing situations that might otherwise lead to open hostilities.

Even Miles Davis, the toughest of the cool cats, the one you would least like to go twelve rounds with (figuratively and literally—as Davis's producer Teo Macero warned journalist Arnold Jay Smith, "Don't let him take you down to his boxing ring; he will hurt you"[1]), made his strongest statements by just walking away. He often turned his back on the audience during a performance or walked off stage when he was done soloing, and this public persona was emblematic of the man's private life. For much of his career, Davis kept as low a profile as possible. The fact that even the feisty Mr. Davis abided, for the most part, by this Gandhi-esque code of behavior tells you how deeply the cool ethos had permeated the trumpeter's personality. In time, not just jazz cats but a whole generation would embrace nonviolence as a core value. Peace and love were not just catchwords for the baby boomers; they were signs of an underlying coolification in the national character.

Further, cool avoided conflict by resisting the pragmatic, by refusing to be results oriented: coolness was an end in itself, not a tool to achieve policies or goals. It was valued intrinsically for what it was, not externally for what rewards it earned. Intrinsic goals were popular with the cool generation—in 1970, 79 percent of college freshmen saw developing a "meaningful philosophy of life" as a key goal. But for the postcool generation, external rewards trump everything. When college freshmen were asked in 2005 to state their primary objective, 75 percent stated it was to be financially well off. While it lasted, this probing within to "find one's self"—for all the ridicule and disbelief it engendered from the older generation—helped cool down the competitive antagonisms that have now jumped to the fore in all spheres of society.[2]

Today, as the cool mind-set is replaced by a new earnestness and directness, differences that once simmered in the background quickly escalate into open confrontation. Postcool prides itself on bluntness and honesty, and though this can sometimes have a tender side—and we will see in the next chapter how this celebration of unfiltered "real" emotion is shaping love songs and other aspects of pop culture—the prevailing communication style these days is more often just plain raw. Even among friends, stylish repartee is out; the brusque text message is in. And between enemies? All disagreements are mano a mano. The pacifying sentiment of "we agree to disagree" has been replaced by "to the victor go the spoils." The signs can be seen everywhere, but nowhere more clearly than in interactive types of media. Just look at talk radio, blogs, online discussion groups, anywhere the audience is invited to share their thoughts, and see how quickly the bombast and nastiness get out of hand. Even traditional one-way media outlets—television, newspapers, magazines, movies—have been caught up in the flaring tempers, and hardly any source of "information" seems able to hold on to a position of neutrality. In the world of modern media, there are no Switzerlands.

A new tone demands a new name, and the word *snark* has rushed in to fill the gap. David Denby, in his 2009 book, *Snark: It's Mean, It's Personal, and It's Ruining Our Conversation*, describes snark as "a strain of nasty, knowing abuse spreading like pinkeye through the national conversation."[3] The term was coined by Lewis Carroll in 1874 (for his poem "The Hunting of the Snark") as a nonsense name combining *snail* and *shark*, and the word lived a quiet life for most of the next century. *Snark* shows up in the 1960s in Richard Crossman's diaries, with echoes of its new meaning, and as the name of a character in Joseph Heller's *Catch-22*. But the golden age of snarkiness would not arrive until the new millennium, when all of a sudden snark was everywhere—and not just the word, even more the behavior it describes.

Yes, there has always been an undercurrent of ugliness in the national dialogue—hate speech, taunting, name-calling—but what sets snark apart from old-fashioned redneck rants is its pervasiveness these days among smart people, opinion leaders, and media celebrities. These are the same folks who, only a few years ago, would have been high-profile advocates for the cool. Indeed, snark is anything but ignorant—it is distinguished by its knowingness, its cultural savvy and intellectual arrogance. It is situated nowadays in the dead center of public discourse and even placed on a stage, holding court wherever one goes. This is a surprising turn of events that could hardly have happened during the Age of Cool, when verbal abusiveness existed but was kept out of the mainstream. If it did show up at a chic event, bystanders were noticeably embarrassed.

Now snark is everywhere. But its most fertile breeding ground is the Internet, where it has become the de facto tone of Web interactivity. If you doubt it, spend some time reading through the comments on a few dozen blog postings and Internet articles, and count the snark attacks. I found this out firsthand, to my amazement and dismay, after launching a jazz website in 2007. I had looked forward to forging a Web community of music fans who would share their enthusiasm for songs and artists, and talk about the music they loved. Instead, a strange crew of nasty, angry people showed up, and their bitterness seemed to spread like wildfire, often chasing away the peaceful music lovers. Perhaps I shouldn't have been surprised—after all, this type of vituperative discourse is all over the Web. But I had thought that jazz fans would be different. Hey, didn't the jazz world invent the cool? Yet the fact that even the present-day disciples of Bix and Prez are hot under the collar tells you how far the cultural tone has drifted.

This same angry polarization is pervasive—and even more destructive—in the world of politics, where moderates are an endangered species. Analyzing the Congress elected in 2006, political scientists Keith T. Poole and Howard Rosenthal determined that it had the fewest percentage of moderates than at any time since the nineteenth century. By their assessment, almost half of the Republicans in Congress in the mid-1970s were moderate, but this

has declined to less than 10 percent during the course of a single
generation. After the 2006 midterm elections, eight of the twenty
most moderate Republicans, as measured by their voting record on
fiscal and social issues, lost their seats.[4] And as Republicans have
become more conservative, Democrats have become more liberal, a
trend furthered by the gradual exodus of conservative southerners
from the party in recent decades. The centrists who once controlled
and softened the rough edges of political debate in Washington
have now abandoned the field, and instead of legislators, we have a
Congress of combatants.

Political campaigns reflect this same polarization and the inevitable aggression that comes with it. Every major election nowadays
is dominated by "gotcha" moments, in which one side catches the
other in a slipup or finds some embarrassing association or past
peccadillo to flaunt in public view. "Gotcha" as a campaign strategy
hardly existed when Dwight Eisenhower ran against Adlai Steven-
son or John F. Kennedy campaigned against Richard Nixon—and
it wasn't because there wasn't dirt to dig up about these candidates.
More to the point, these earlier elections had not yet descended
into the gutters for constant ad hominem attacks. But nowadays,
whenever a major election approaches, every day is a gotcha day for
both sides in the contest. The journalists on the political beat hover
over these "revelations" with the tenacity of vultures circling the site
of a massacre.

Yet if one is pressed to find anticool at its highest pitch, the
place to look (or rather, to listen) is obvious: talk radio. Rush Limbaugh is to James Dean what antimatter is to matter. Any measure
of coolness coefficient would have put folks like Bill O'Reilly and
Michael Savage into remedial classes before they entered preschool.
These cats are not cool. Just check out the biographies of these stars
and see where they came from (Limbaugh, by his own mother's
admission, failed everything at Southeast Missouri State, even ball-
room dancing)—but they got to the top of their profession through
sheer cussedness and a will to dominate. Nor is it just the right side
of the political spectrum that has lost its cool. Masters of confrontation from the left, such as Michael Moore and Al Franken, won't
be showing up on the cover of *GQ* any time soon. They will never
appear in a Gap ad for khakis. They won't have a line of cologne put
out under their imprimatur.

The fact that this stomp-on-your-enemies tone is so popular
with the general public is a telling indicator of the modern American Zeitgeist. And what do we see when we look at the audience—
measuring in the tens of millions—of these hard-nosed pundits?

I'll tell you what we see…a lot of very angry people sitting by their radio sets or televisions or broadband Internet hookups. Sad to say, the short-tempered hosts are often calmer than the people who call in to their shows. What's going on here?

Look around you; anger is big business these days. Anger management hardly existed as a discipline before the nineties, but today it is one of the fastest-growing professions. When Dr. Steven Stosny started his anger-focused counseling practice in 1990, his patients were maximum-security inmates. But today he has found that the demand for his services crosses over into all demographic groups. Once it was just the felon who needed his services; today it might be the corporate executive on the go or your next-door neighbor. Stosny has been a regular visitor to *The Oprah Winfrey Show*, and has trained one thousand workshop leaders, who have shared his branded techniques all over the world.

The range of products and services in this booming mini-industry testifies how pervasive angry confrontation has become in modern life. There are anger-management home-study courses, boot camps, DVDs, online tutorials, court-mandated activities, personal coaching, telecounseling, workplace interventions, school-based training, twelve-step programs, one-on-one therapies, you name it. And the programs multiply faster than Amway or Mary Kay schemes—at angerbusters.com, you can learn how to become a certified anger-management counselor after only two days of training.

The signs of our escalating temper are everywhere. If hip was the emerging personality style of the fifties and sixties, anger has become the defining attitude of the nineties and new millennium. Around 1997, therapists began advocating that road rage be considered a medical condition. Two decades before, the term didn't even exist. About this same time, air rage—outbursts by unruly passengers on flights—became increasingly evident. Although reliable statistics are not available, R. C. Costa Pereira, former secretary-general of the International Civil Aviation Organization (ICAO), has noted that incidents seemed to increase markedly after the midnineties. British railway stations now have signs asking passengers to refrain from assaulting the staff, and the London Underground has also posted notices telling the once well-mannered travelers not to push each other, to allow people to get on and off, and so forth.

What happened to the British decorum and the stiff upper lip? Michael Deacon, writing in *The Telegraph* on New Year's Day in 2009, asks, "What's next, 'Please Don't Steal,' 'Please Try Not to Kill

Each Other'?" He proposes a resolution for the new year: could we be a little more polite, please? But even Deacon is not optimistic, noting that rudeness is "no longer something to be ashamed of; it's applauded."[5] He notes that more than one million people have joined a Facebook group called "I Secretly Want To Punch Slow Walking People In The Back Of The Head."

Other bizarre yet revealing terminologies entered the vocabulary during the new millennium. Members of my parents' generation would have laughed at the notion of wrap rage, which refers to the anger of consumers who struggle to extract a product from its packaging, or computer rage, which identifies out-of-control frustration aimed at a fickle desktop or laptop unit. But terms such as these are now commonly tossed about, as is that amusing if alarming description of a disgruntled employee "going postal"—an idiom that didn't exist before 1993. A catchall diagnosis of Intermittent Explosive Disorder (IED) is now increasingly applied to such behavior patterns. A study conducted by Harvard University in 2006 suggested that as many as one in every fourteen adults is afflicted with this disorder.[6]

Even people who hold their anger and snarkiness in check apparently enjoy seeing others let it rip. Almost every so-called reality show these days needs some blunt and callous figure to dish out the dirt. Donald Trump's caustic rejoinder "You're fired!" soon became such a popular part of *The Apprentice* that he filed to trademark the phrase. When I was growing up, Julia Child was the queen of culinary decorum in the media and the Galloping Gourmet, Graham Kerr, prepared his dishes with constant light-hearted banter and tomfoolery, but the representative TV chef of the current age is Gordon Ramsay, whose various cooking shows have more bleeped-out bad language than the rap CD section at Walmart. Yet the king of the rude rejoinder is clearly Simon Cowell of *American Idol*, whose philosophy is apparently: "If you don't have something good to say about someone, let's broadcast it on TV." How important are Cowell's blunt takedowns to the show's success? One can measure it by the disparity in salaries between Paula Abdul, the nurturing judge on the show, who reportedly earns around $2 million per year from *American Idol*, and Cowell, who takes home a whopping $36 million (not including his cut from records made by contestants). What does it say about the psyche of our times if, in this game of good cop/bad cop, the latter gets almost all the spoils?

This is the dark, ugly side of postcool society. Cool was not perfect: its posturing, its aloofness, its preference for irony over earnestness, its obsession with style over substance…these were its limitations and blind spots. But cool didn't like ugly scenes or temper tantrums or the infantile rage that is now coming to the fore in society. Civil life is no longer quite so civil, and the death of the cool has been a major contributor to the nastiness around us.

Perhaps all this aggression will eventually burn itself out. Any student of Darwinian processes in social life knows that a kind of karma eventually comes to rule in modern societies. Those who bully and intimidate and try to dominate rarely last for long. American society may be delighted for the present with the bare-knuckled exchanges that pass for democracy, but I have a hunch that this fascination with blood sport in the realm of public policy won't last forever. In fact, this might be the reason why postcool itself will eventually be superseded by its own replacement, just as it dislodged the cool cats.

The Sound of Postcool Music

Here are the rules of our imaginary essay contest. Predict the next eighty years of development in the arts in eighty words or less. Winners will be announced sometime in your grandchildren's lifetime. Tough assignment, eh?

Let's see how a discerning mind handled the task in 1925. Here is José Ortega y Gasset, the great Spanish philosopher and one of the most acute critical minds of the early twentieth century, from his essay "The Dehumanization of Art":

> When we analyze the new style we find that it contains certain closely connected tendencies. It tends (1) to dehumanize art, (2) to avoid living forms, (3) to see to it that the work of art is nothing but a work of art, (4) to consider art as play and nothing else, (5) to be essentially ironical, (6) to beware of sham and hence to aspire to scrupulous realization, (7) to regard art as a thing of no transcending consequence.[1]

What are we to make of this grand prognostication, this seven-step program for the next new thing? The visual arts were perhaps Ortega's primary concern here. His first two points stand out as a direct response to the tendency toward abstraction gaining momentum at the time he wrote—but the next five items on the list are even more prescient, anticipating in large part what would happen after the shift to abstraction had played out its course, serving in short as a recipe for art during the Age of Cool. In stunning anticipation of later events, Ortega's recipe outlines tendencies that would sweep through virtually all genres, altering most forms of cultural expression. So much of our contemporary scene is foreshadowed in these words: the merging and confusion of highbrow and lowbrow styles; the dominance of entertainment over art; the advancement of linguistic models that see all cultural products as "texts" and "signifiers" dissociated from the artists who originally shaped them; and above all the recurring ironical stance that has increasingly dominated public discourse during the last half century.

Ortega's formula would seem to have the least relevance to music, a mode of expression that has always been abstract, intangible, disembodied almost by definition. His descriptors seem especially out of touch with the modern music of the early twentieth century. The compositions of Schoenberg, Stravinsky, Bartók, Strauss, Webern, and Copland strike many listeners as deadly serious, perhaps even gloomy. Only the more discerning ear picks out the elements of playfulness and irony highlighted by Ortega— although probably more easily today than when these works were first performed. But fast-forward to the second half of the century, and everyone from John Adams to John Zorn seems to have adopted a piquant postmodern stance, to have accepted Ortega's list as a code of core values. The relationship between the composer and the composition had once seemed nonproblematic—music, after all, was a form of expression, heartfelt and sincere. Or was it? As the century grew older, albeit not necessarily wiser, the view of music as a direct, expressive activity began to seem quaint and naive, at best a carryover from nineteenth-century Romanticism, at worst pure balderdash that had never been true.

The more fascinating story, in my opinion, is how even the teenagers and mall rats got co-opted, how this ironical stance came to dominate popular music. In my grandparents' day, popular music resisted irony. It embraced sentimentality—irony's opposite, irony's foe. When cool came to the fore, during the middle of the twentieth century, this unabashed sentimentality was one of the first things it threw overboard. We may laugh today (with ironic superiority, needless to say) at the popular music of earlier generations—"Sweet Adeline," "Home on the Range" (FDR's favorite song), "After the Ball," "Beautiful Dreamer," and the like. We may accuse it of phoniness or vapidity. We may criticize its banalities, point out its stereotypes, and parody its clichés. But these responses tell us more about our own preconceptions, our own biases, than inform us about how these songs were heard by their intended audience.

The people who wrote this sentimental music hoped to pull on the heartstrings of the American public, and their success— financially, certainly, and even artistically, at least from their own perspective—was based on this emotional appeal. The potency of the music was inextricably linked to the power of the feelings it elicited. From the exclamation point in the title of "Oh! Susanna" to the sleigh bells in the snow in "White Christmas," this music may have been a bunch of commercial constructs tied together with maudlin images, but it always strove to appear as something warmer and deeper. The tunesmiths hoped that audiences wouldn't notice the sham—the "suspension of disbelief" is what the experts called it in a kindler and gentler age—that they would buy into the sentiments, and maybe even shed a tear.

A few years later, everything had changed. In the Age of Cool, these songs might still find an appreciative audience, but—and this is all too revealing—almost exclusively with very young children. They would sing Stephen Foster songs such as "Oh! Susanna" at school and buy into the emotionalism, much as the toddler joins in when Barney the dinosaur belts out his anthem: "I LOVE you, you LOVE me. We're a happy family." For grown-ups, direct and nonironic expression of deeply felt tenderness in songs made them feel uncomfortable. In the modern era, even pop songs, tradition-ally built and sold on sentiment, were suspect if their emotional message was too direct. This marked the final (albeit temporary) triumph of irony, the capture of a territory that would by nature have resisted its onslaught.

This transformation did not happen overnight, and the songs put up a valiant fight. The sentimental undercurrent in popular music proved very resilient, and for one simple reason. In free and open societies, pop music is inevitably dominated by love songs. Why? Perhaps Darwin got it right when he claimed that music developed and evolved because of its use in courtship and mating. His evidence is scanty, and he pays more attention to birdsongs than to human music in making his point. But the evidence on the airwaves is undeniable. Listen to music on the radio for an hour, or listen for a whole week (if you can stand it). Dig into the archives of Casey Kasem with the vigilance of Heinrich Schliemann uncover-ing the ruins of Troy. Love is all around you, my friend. Happy love, sad love, puppy love, dirty love. Wherever you turn the dial, there you find it.

This time-honored association of popular music with romance and courtship placed a major obstacle in the paths of the cool ironists...at least at first. Romance forces us to lower our guard; coolness requires that we raise it. Something had to give here, and the love song was where the battle was played out. Romance and sentimentality put up a fight, but they were doomed to eventual failure in an age dominated by the cool. By necessity, even love songs now needed to find a way to be ironic and aloof, but at what a cost! An ironic attitude to love is possible, but hardly desirable—

unless you've spent too much time on eHarmony.com lately—and it is a struggle to maintain. Just gaze at the sappy looks on the faces in the wedding announcement photos in the *The New York Times.* If New Yorkers, who master a tough gaze by age seven, can end up looking like that, what hope is there for the rest of us?

Yes, even the love song was transformed by the cool, an event that should have been heralded in town squares, proclaimed from the rooftops, as when Alaric stormed Rome or the Saracens cordoned off Jerusalem. But it happened so gradually that almost nobody noticed. As with so many cultural trends, the fifties saw the first stirrings of the new style that would become a dominant strain in the sixties and seventies. With the benefit of hindsight, we can identify the pop music figure who destroyed the old paradigm and made way for the emerging cool tone in American music: Frank Sinatra.

No one had sung pop music with such an *attitude* before. No one had mastered, like Sinatra, the ability to sing a tune and also provide color commentary along the way, impishly making fun of the very song he was performing. Today we talk glibly of a singer *interpreting* a song, but even this modern perspective is our legacy from Sinatra. Before Sinatra, singers tried to *inhabit* the song. Look at Al Jolson on his knee with outstretched arms, shouting to the back row, tears glistening in his eyes, and you get a sense of how much baggage Sinatra had to toss overboard in reconfiguring the American popular song. Above all, Sinatra disdained emotional excess. He taught us that a pop star needs to adopt a perspective, take a view, play a role. And just as modern literary critics remind us that there are an infinite number of ways of interpreting a text, so Sinatra showed that the possible perspectives on a tune were as numerous as angels on the head of a pin. What an intoxicating concept for a singer! Before Sinatra there was only one approach, an unapologetic immediacy, a salubrious thrusting of the performer into the persona of the song, as invigorating and scary as a plunge into cold waters. But after Sinatra, a thousand and one personas were available for the taking, a different one each night, if you will. And a thousand and one more were waiting in the wings.

Chalk this up as one of the Chairman of the Board's greatest achievements—less well known, certainly, than his Oscar and ten Grammy statuettes, but even more lasting in its impact. Sinatra was our Derrida of the hit parade. He was our postmodernist of the microphone, who did to Cole Porter and George Gershwin what Roland Barthes did to Honoré de Balzac's "Sarrasine" in *S/Z.* While others sang love songs, Sinatra deconstructed them.

In an earlier day, the public would have felt shortchanged. After all, this upstart was taking the romance out of love songs. But here Sinatra proved to be a sociologist as acute as that other Hoboken lad, Alfred Kinsey, as adept in understanding the shifting sands of American views on the relations between the sexes. I sometimes fantasize about a hypothetical meeting between these two Jersey natives, perhaps over dinner at the Clam Broth House, in which the older sexologist passes on words of wisdom to the young crooner, telling him to find inspiration for his songs not in his heart but in a region some fifty centimeters closer to the clamshell-littered floor. But Kinsey left Hoboken a few months before Sinatra was born. So there was no meeting, and I can do no better than give a nod to the singer's own shrewd assessment of the American public. He didn't need Kinsey; he had figured it out for himself.

The new generation wanted titillation, not pledges of undying love. Just as the institutions of monogamy would change in the face of this onslaught, so would the pop songs. Sinatra was the first to recognize it. The old songs could not be sung straight anymore. They needed to be modernized, just as the Louvre required a large glass pyramid in front of its entrance—otherwise the weight of tradition was just too damn heavy (as Sinatra, the great pioneer in bringing swear words into pop music, might say), the claims of the old-fashioned ways too much for us to bear.

Perhaps the best way of measuring this change is to compare Sinatra with Billie Holiday. Holiday was only eight months older than Sinatra, but she represents a style of singing that might as well be from a different generation, or even century. Until the end of her life, Holiday held true to the view that the singer must live the song, must enter into its heart and soul fully and completely. Any distance from the core feelings of the lyrics is a form of dishonesty. And Holiday's greatness as a vocalist derives almost entirely from this one intangible metric, her refusal to be dishonest, her insistence on preserving the core emotional truth of the song. Her range was limited, her memory for lyrics faulty, her reliability on the gig suspect, the power of her vocal cords no match for a Bessie Smith or Sophie Tucker. But we hear her voice and are overpowered and overawed by the sheer verisimilitude and believability of what she sings.

The hypertrophied sense of irony developed by Sinatra in the fifties would become the dominant tone in the sixties and seventies, and not just (or even primarily) in the world of cabaret and lounge singers. The rock revolution borrowed from Sinatra long before Sid Vicious covered "My Way," although the transition took place in fits and starts. In The Beatles, John Lennon adopted the new ironic worldview, while Paul McCartney stayed true to the older tradition of heartfelt singing. Yet Mick Jagger may have represented the purest version of the Sinatra ethos, parading and posing on stage, celebrating his own cult of personality no matter what the ostensible subject of the song might be. Here was the modern entertainer in all his glory, and his role was no longer to help the audience enter into the fantasy of the song. No, not at all. The audience now wanted to fantasize about what it was like to be a bigger-than-life rock star, with all the perks. In this light, the lyrics were irrelevant. Jagger might as well be singing nonsense syllables—and, indeed, sometimes they sounded just like that. (Even the most devoted fans failed to decipher the lyrics to "Tumbling Dice" until Linda Ronstadt covered the song in 1978. And Ronstadt needed to get Jagger to write down the words, since nobody in her band could figure out what the hell he was singing.) But if the strut and gestures were right, if the air was thick with glamour and stardom, then nothing else really mattered. Other rock stars of the era jumped on the bandwagon, and in time metaphorical glitter was no longer enough, as artists as diverse as Kiss and Elton John reached out for whatever costumes, makeup, or props that would accentuate their exalted cool station above it all, keeping them out of touch with the gritty emotions of real day-to-day life.

By now, the new cool tone was permeating every aspect of popular culture, and not just music. The mini-industry of comedy was perhaps the most revealing, as it always is, of the hidden psychological shifts inside the American cranium, and here countless examples testified to the death of the old school.

Red Skelton had been a preeminent television star until his demographics (in the parlance of the industry) with younger viewers collapsed at the end of the sixties, and his failure tells us much about what modern Americans no longer found funny. Skelton was the son of a circus clown who died shortly before the youngster's birth in 1913 in Vincennes, Indiana. During his formative years, Skelton mastered the full range of traditional American comedy as it existed in these precool days: he too worked as a circus clown and learned the subtleties of entertaining audiences in medicine shows and minstrel groups, on showboats and vaudeville stages, eventually working his way into motion pictures and radio. His homespun humor resonated with the heartstrings of Middle America: a typical routine found him engaging in an elaborate pantomime of the onlookers' reactions at a small-town parade when the American flag passes by. He kept faith in the oldest comedic devices—miming, pratfalls, the double take, long-winded stories—but most memorable were his characters, the seagulls, Gertrude and Heathcliffe, and especially the country bumpkin, Clem Kadiddlehopper. Through it all, Skelton did something very rare, especially in the comedic arts: he came across as kind and warmhearted, somehow countering the inherent harshness of humor with a benevolence that endeared him to his audiences.

Or at least for a time. The phenomenal success that brought Skelton to the summit of the television world faltered in the face of the changing tastes and new attitudes of the oh-so-cool late sixties. CBS executives dropped him from their lineup in 1970, fed up with his salary demands and sensitive to his poor ratings among the highly coveted under-thirty audience, which, according to the conventional wisdom of the time, was the only group you could trust. Two years earlier, Dan Rowan and Dick Martin had turned TV comedy upside down with the hour-long *Laugh-In* show, which quickly established itself as the leader in the ratings war. Rowan and Martin disdained storytelling, miming, clowning, and, in short, all the things Skelton represented, in favor of rapid-fire wisecracks and ironic put-downs, verbal humor and innuendo, performed by a large ensemble of regulars including Goldie Hawn, Lily Tomlin, Arte Johnson, and Ruth Buzzi. An ultracool atmosphere pervaded *Laugh-In*—in fact, a recurring segment featured the whole cast at a stylish cocktail party exchanging can-you-outhip-this witticisms. Television viewers now wanted, it seems, to maximize the punch lines, minimize the setup. Skits on *Laugh-In* might last only a few seconds, just enough to make way for a zinger. Skelton seemed slow and stodgy by comparison, a carryover from a bygone era. The NBC network picked him up after CBS dropped his show, but he was now booked immediately before *Laugh-In*, on the same network and out of place on Rowan and Martin's Monday-night turf. One might as well have asked Bing Crosby to sing as warm-up act for The Mothers of Invention. Needless to say, Skelton failed badly in this lineup, and the new show was dropped after a single season.

Meanwhile, back in Skelton's Indiana, another comedian was honing his craft and paying close attention to the ironic and absurdist tendencies coming to the fore in contemporary comedy. David Letterman would eventually rise to fame on the same NBC network that had refined the harder *Laugh-In* approach, but Letterman would adopt an even more deconstructive attitude. If *Laugh-In* renounced storytelling in favor of just punch lines, Letterman found that he could often even dispense with the punch line. A mere verbal inflection, a smirk, a clichéd phrase offered with multiple layers of sarcasm, an attitude, a rolling of the eyes—these were perfectly sufficient for his needs. His comedy was built on the coolly aloof premise that the world itself was ridiculous: all he needed to do was gaze at it with the right supercilious look and everyone would get the joke and start laughing. He delighted in real-life segments, going out on the street, making semirandom phone calls, enlisting stagehands and urban neighbors as collaborators, all based on the sense of inherent comedy in modern-day America. At its best, his wit was devastating; he knew exactly where to find the absurdist underside of everyday things. Yet no comedian had ever been colder, less endearing. If Skelton was the last of the humorists to exude genuine warmth, Letterman resided at the opposite extreme. His humor was so cool it was almost covered in a polar frost.

I dwell on this shift at some length because the path of American comedy in these years most clearly shows the overall cultural transformation, the cooling—perhaps it is better to say the chilling—of the modern mind. And the emergence of postcool is now reshaping comedy, as gags and pratfalls and goofiness have come back in full force. I could give many examples, and not just the current crop of goofmeisters who have appeared in the wake of Jim Carrey, or even those such as Eddie Murphy who turbocharged their careers by renouncing edgy cool in favor of warm-and-fuzzy postcool. But the most revealing fact of all comes from a John Zogby December 2006 survey in which the famous pollster asked a random sample of roughly four thousand respondents, "Who do you consider to be the funniest comedic performer of all time?" The biggest vote-getter was…Red Skelton. *Red Skelton*? A decade after his death and thirty-six years after his TV show was canceled because of lousy ratings, this most uncool of the comedians rises to the top of the heap? Bill Cosby, that other paragon of precool comedy styles, finished in second place.[2] And, as we saw back in Chapter One, a host of other comedic minds are noticing the shift to a new naturalism in the world of comedy. What's going on here?

Clearly something strange and unexpected is taking place deep in the crevices of the modern mind. Among *Homo sapiens*, no social response is more raw and revealing than laughter. What people find funny gives us an unfiltered glimpse of what is going on in their psyches. Long before attitudinal changes are articulated in concepts and principles, they show up in a chuckle and guffaw. When people's tastes in humor change, be on the lookout for a similar shift in other aspects of their lives.

The public's taste in music has followed the exact same path as that outlined in the world of comedy, but at a slower pace. Despite the examples set by Sinatra, Jagger, Lennon, and others, the cool attitude only gradually took over the pop charts. The same audience that embraced irony and distance in its humor during the fifties and sixties at first resisted these same acidic qualities in popular music. The natural tendency to seek warmth and shelter in the amorous strains of a love song was so deeply ingrained that it took a whole generation before the emerging popular styles broke completely free from the sentimental and heartfelt, before we achieved a hit parade largely purged of intimate emotional feelings.

Even as late as the seventies, the singer-songwriters continued to offer a softer side of pop-rock, summoning up intimate, confessional ballads, often performed unadorned and unplugged in simple onstage arrangements, perhaps one or two guitars or with simple piano or small combo backing. No, Stephen Foster had not come back to life; yet, when James Taylor played "Oh! Susanna," he sang it straight and with feeling, and the distance between the old sentimentalists and the new acoustic performers didn't seem like such a big gulf after all. For more than a decade following the arrival of Bob Dylan, music listeners were engaged by an endless variety of these singer-songwriters, a veritable golden age of heart-on-your-sleeve pop music: Joni Mitchell, Cat Stevens, James Taylor, Carole King, Laura Nyro, John Denver, Gordon Lightfoot, Neil Young, Jim Croce, Neil Diamond, Carly Simon, Nick Drake, Van Morrison, Roberta Flack, Harry Chapin, and many others embraced a light, bittersweet, confessional style, emotionally direct and intimate. Their records sold in enormous quantities, and even the most scornful hard-rock fans—who tended to look down on this music, sometimes ridiculing it outright for its sentimental qualities—accepted that it was a permanent part of the music scene, destined to account for a significant portion of the nation's record sales.

But in the midseventies, Elton John left the singer-songwriter camp and embraced glitter rock with a vengeance. The dreamy-eyed balladeer who had first hit the big time with "Your Song," a sweet love ballad presented in a stark, piano-based arrangement, now came out of the closet as Captain Fantastic, with outlandish outfits, over-the-top makeup and props, and a pull-out-all-the-stops road entourage. No one actually posted an obituary notice for the singer-songwriter category in *Billboard* magazine, but then again it wasn't necessary. Record sales plummeted for even the leaders of the movement. Carole King dominated the charts in 1970, her *Tapestry* selling more than twenty million copies worldwide, but by 1975 she was struggling to get airplay. A chasm had seemingly opened up in a California earthquake and sucked down Roberta

Flack and Cat Stevens and Gilbert O'Sullivan and Don McLean and a bunch of others, never again to be heard from by top-forty fans. Almost all of the singer-songwriters experienced a painful retrenching, a ratcheting down in share price, as the public demonstrated that it was just as fickle as the lovers celebrated in these songs, renouncing a style that, only a short while before, had promised to last forever. Just a handful of this endangered breed survived, and these were (no surprise here) the most ironic of the singer-songwriter bunch—Randy Newman, Billy Joel, Paul Simon—those, in short, most adaptable to the new order of things, those who had never built their music on sweet love songs in the first place.

The disappearance of the singer-songwriter was not a healthy long-term development for the recording industry. And the rise of the music video a few years later hammered the nails even more firmly into the coffin, building careers around how artists *looked* and *danced* instead of how well they *composed* and *played* music. It was almost as if the music industry had a death instinct, wanting to become an ultracool glamour and fashion business, in thrall to images rather than to (its core strength since the beginning of time) sounds. But the shift in attitude of these transitional years, before the rise of MTV, was not without its benefits. The delicate balance—and sometimes the outright battle—between the ironic and the heartfelt made for some of the most exciting music of the sixties and seventies. Who can deny that this yin and yang contrast between Lennon and McCartney contributed markedly to the allure of The Beatles? We saw the same thing with Simon and Garfunkel, Rowan and Martin, Captain Kirk and Mr. Spock, Nixon and Ford, Charlie Brown and Lucy—emotive immediacy and supercilious distance playing off each other in a psychological dance that defined the era. Ah, the Age of Cool was a great time to write music, a creative tension was in the air...at least until the ironists won the war, the Spocks took over the *Starship Enterprise* and beamed the Kirks out to the far reaches of the galaxy, never to be heard from again.

Around the same time that the singer-songwriter was sent into exile, new forms of popular expression were rising. The term *punk rock* didn't even exist when *Tapestry* was on top of the charts, but by the middle of the decade this hyperaggressive sound was shaking up the club scene in New York and other major cities. Punk ran roughshod over everything that traditional pop music had represented. If pop was bittersweet, punk was merely bitter. If pop embraced love as its guiding light, punk offered frustration, anger, discontent, aggression, and a bad attitude married to a bad haircut. If pop offered sweetness and light, punk preached nihilism and anarchy.

If pop had been built on Tin Pan Alley craftsmanship, careful constructions of harmony, melody, and rhythm, then punk was deconstruction, knocking down these careful edifices in a torrent of noisy, electric sound sludge.

If you had any doubts that this new music took pride in being rotten and vicious, you just needed to look at its most famous early exponents, who even changed their names to Rotten and Vicious. *Rolling Stone*, in its review of the Sex Pistols' *Never Mind the Bollocks*, characterized the sound of the music as "two subway trains crashing together under forty feet of mud, victims scream- ing"—and, yes, this was a *positive* review by an astute critic in touch with the modern sensibility. In short, punk was the perfect soundtrack for the times, a performance style that fulfilled Orte- ga's prediction of a half century before, his vision of art stripped of its humanizing veneer.

Again, irony was the guiding light of this music. If the Sex Pistols released their recording of "God Save the Queen" to coincide with the Queen's silver jubilee, one could be certain that no touching tribute to enduring monarchy was intended, only a snide, above-it-all put-down. Traditional institutions of this sort, of course, were essential to the punk ethos—its spirit was so corrosive, it constantly required new idols to topple, taboos to violate, and ways of focusing its otherwise meaningless energy. Sid Vicious of the Sex Pistols was the perfect hero for the movement, celebrated by his fans for legendary exploits that symbolized the new nihil- istic mind-set. The day his band was signed to A&M Records, he trashed the office of the label's managing director and left behind a pile of vomit on the boss's desk. A&M mopped up the mess... and pulled out of the deal, but Virgin stepped in to promote what would become the most influential music act of its day. Vicious, for his part, would go on to destroy many other things much more valuable than a music mogul's office, including, some suspect, his girlfriend Nancy Spungen, who died from a stab wound in 1978, and finally himself, from an overdose the following year.

Unlike the Pistols' version of "God Save the Queen," Vicious's rendition of Sinatra's "My Way" did not require a reconfiguration of the song's basic tone. Sinatra had created, in this paean to self-ac- tualization, a solipsistic tribute to ego run rampant that perfectly suited the punk revolution. Vicious merely tried to step into Sina- tra's shoes and assert that his way was just as good as Frank's way. If any had doubted that Sinatra was ahead of his time, a harbinger of the postromantic, ironic school of antipop, here was proof positive. But even Vicious could not top the Chairman of the Board, and almost as if to reassert his timeliness and supremacy, Sinatra hit the charts shortly after Vicious's passing. In an over-the-top version of "New York, New York," he celebrated, at age sixty-five, his triumph over the same city that proved too much for Sid and Nancy. Sinatra's tremendous popularity, at an age when few pop sensations retain much of an audience, was no fluke. He had laid the groundwork for everything that was happening in contemporary commercial music, purging the popular song of its sentimental traditions and preparing the world for the new cool order of things. He had earned this acclaim.

But the emergence of punk rock was only one sign among many that the age of intimacy and romance had ended on the airwaves. Other new-wave performers, from the Talking Heads to Devo, offered equally irony-infused perspectives on contemporary culture. Heavy metal, satanic rock, disco, and other styles mounted the same war on different terrains, each taking a scorched earth approach to the emotional landscape. The black music scene followed a similar path, renouncing the warmth of soul music in favor of the harshness of rap. Everywhere one turned the radio dial, the same phenomenon was playing out, a hardening of the emotional arteries, singers who were above it all, copping a never-ending attitude. No vulnerabilities or moments of self-doubt were allowed scope for expression. The idealization of "the other," the guiding light of popular music since time immemorial, now gave way to the celebration of ego and a petrifying of the heart.

But like all dominant styles, this one, too, was destined, in its turn, to come to an end. Some might have thought that the old precool ways would never come back, that, like losing your virginity, the innocence of the heartfelt love song could never be regained once forfeited. The masters of the new world order assumed that, once the corrosive and deconstructive attitude had gained ascendancy, it would destroy all other contenders; its nihilism would prove irresistible. Because, after all, it is far simpler to tear down an edifice than to build one, easier to critique than construct. After the Sex Pistols and X-rated rap and death metal and everything else, who would even dare try to reclaim this neighborhood with a sweet love song?

Yes, it is easier to deface and destroy your hood than build something solid. But in the world of *human* affairs—and especially in popular music—the opposite is sometimes true: people need sustenance and nutrition, and they will toil year-round to raise a crop if that is the only way they can eat. And emotional sustenance is almost as important as food. Irony makes for a poor diet: the limbs weaken, the digestive track rebels, and the culture that is fed on it for too long grows sickly and eventually dies. The ironic style was anything but sustainable. It would inevitably be rejected. The only question was when and how.

The first glimmerings of the postironic age in music could be seen in the eighties with the surprising and almost shocking arrival of New Age music, a style of performance that not only had no attitude, but even seemed to believe that it represented something authentic and deep. This seriousness was, of course, met with ridicule by almost everyone else. The conventional view held that the New Agers were hopelessly naive, duped members of a bogus cult. How dare they believe that music had some transcendent purpose! Such earnestness had not been seen in the world of commercial music for decades, and, according to the best-received opinions, it should be sent packing immediately.

Yet listeners responded to this music with a fervor that was extraordinary, especially when compared with the placidity of the recordings themselves. I recall a disc jockey at a local jazz station telling me how the programming director had mistakenly placed a George Winston track into rotation. He didn't understand the emerging New Age sound and thought that Winston was a jazz musician—an easy mistake to make, since his piano style came across as a watered-down version of Keith Jarrett's solo recordings from the period. But fans heard the difference. Whenever the Winston recording played, the phones rang off the hook at the station. No, the calls did not come from angry fans demanding their jazz back, but rather from enthusiastic listeners who absolutely had to know the name of the record on the air so they could rush out to buy it. How did the programming director react to this unanticipated success? My deejay friend summed up the resolution to the story in a few words: "We took care of that. We made sure never to play those records again."

Indeed, the whole music industry made the same vow, but to no avail. The power brokers, not having a financial stake in the music, were indifferent or often actively hostile to its inroads. Despite this cold shoulder from the custodians of cool, the New Age recordings found distribution in places that the major labels didn't even know existed—health food stores, vitamin shops, art galleries, yoga studios, and the like. This should come as no surprise to the readers of this book, however: these same locations have served as breeding grounds, as we have seen, for many aspects of the postcool ethos. But to an exec at an entertainment conglomerate back in the 1980s, the idea that you could sell lots of CDs by promoting them alongside massage oils and antioxidant vitamins was a revelation. Lacking powerful partners in radio or retail, the New Age artists found their audience through word of mouth, unpaid proselytizing, and, above all, through in-store play at these alternative outlets. Sometimes the store owners would play these same recordings over and over all day long—a degree of promotion that could never be achieved in a record store, where the turntable turnover was nonstop—and displayed the discs prominently on their checkout counters. Shoppers took notice and bought the releases from Windham Hill and the other start-up labels in prodigious quantities.

Much of this music was almost mindlessly simple, the musicians often amateurish in their technical command of their instruments, the pieces built around the limitations rather than the visionary ambitions of the composer. Schooled in my own jazz-oriented value system, I dismissed much of it at the time as sonic pablum, suitable only for those unable to digest stronger fare. Even today, I find most of it unlistenable. Yet the sudden, rapid expansion of the audience for these recordings was, in many ways, more important than the music itself. It revealed not just the market demand, but even more the deep-felt hunger of the contemporary listener who craved something more intimate, more authentic than the cold and ironic songs that dominated the airwaves. New Age music only seldom achieved this depth and meaning, but that should not blind us to the very real malaise that New Age fans sensed on the radio, at the nightclubs, and in the record stores.

But in time other signs of the death, or at least increasing frailty, of the ironic tone in music would appear. Movie soundtrack music had never successfully succumbed to it in the first place—music's role here was clearly to reinforce the emotional changes of the story, and no scope was allowed for wavering or doubt—and now it was rewarded for its fidelity to the old values. As cool started to collapse, not only did the megahits, such as *Titanic* and *Forrest Gump*, find a ready audience for their scores (that had always been the case for these star-laden LPs), but even fringe music from a cult film could top the charts, as demonstrated when the soundtrack to *O Brother, Where Art Thou?* sold seven million units and walked away with a Grammy for record of the year—with a mix of work songs, old folk tunes, and gospel that seemed distinctly noncommercial. This was music for your dead great-grandpa…and it was the biggest hit of the year. A surprise? Perhaps for the music industry, but for those who sensed the audience's craving for something more heartfelt than gangsta rap and death metal, the runaway success of such projects made perfect sense.

Perhaps most revealing of the new earnestness that was coming to define postcool music, the older artists who had never had a knack for irony and were often ridiculed for sticking so doggedly to the surface meaning in lyrics suddenly found themselves in demand again. When I went to see Tony Bennett performing at San Francisco's Fairmont Hotel in the mideighties, I noticed with some discomfort that I was the youngest person in the room. Of course, I knew that Bennett was unfashionable—at the close of the seventies he had no record contract, no manager, and he struggled to generate concert bookings outside of the Las Vegas casinos that catered to stars of his sort on the downward slope of their careers. His last hit was almost twenty years old, and no one thought there was much of a chance for another one, not now, not ever. The only dedicated Tony Bennett fan I knew was my father, and among music fans my own age the singer was perceived as hopelessly square. After all, he sang love songs as if he meant them, like he actually believed the sappy words, the hackneyed sentiments. Like a grad student in an English class who actually thought that *Moby Dick* was about fishing, that *Hamlet* was about the succession issue in Denmark, Bennett came across as a simpleton who missed the multiple layers of meaning inherent in any "text." Not only wasn't he cool; he was the antithesis of everything hip and modern.

Only a year before I saw Bennett, Woody Allen had presented a parody of a washed-up Italian American singer, Lou Canova, in the movie *Broadway Danny Rose*. Canova was a sap who sang with his heart on his sleeve and came across as all the more comic for channeling his emotions into these tunes in such an uncomplicated manner. The message here was clear: like the youngster who believes in the tooth fairy or the Easter Bunny, the singer who accepted the magic of these tunes at face value merely showed naivete. The character of Canova struck me as loosely based on Bennett, who now had gone from being merely unfashionable to the actual butt of a joke. No wonder I was a statistical outlier at the Fairmont that night.

But the artist who was too old-fashioned at age sixty was on top of the world at age seventy—and, marvel of marvels, with an audience young enough to be his grandchildren. Signed once again by Columbia, the label that had scorned him just a few years before, Bennett started to find a new fan base at the close of the eighties. But the floodgates burst open with his "unplugged" performance on MTV in 1994, which caused extraordinary hubbub and, in the words of industry executives, market expansion. The resulting recording, *MTV Unplugged: Tony Bennett*, went platinum, earned the top Grammy honor for album of the year, and became the best seller of the singer's career. Moreover, Bennett achieved this without making a single change in the cabaret style he had been perfecting for decades. "I've always been unplugged," he quipped, and the song mix he chose for his young fans drew unapologetically on the works of Irving Berlin, George Gershwin, Cole Porter, Duke Ellington, and other tunesmiths from the pre-cool era. Bennett had stayed cussedly in one place and waited for the audience to come to him…and it did!

But Bennett was far from the only example of this surprising turnabout. Young fans sought out precisely those older singers who had the least amount of postmodern irony in their interpretations—Johnny Cash, Ray Charles, B. B. King, even Barry Manilow, the king of schmaltz. And artists who had made their name as supreme ironists dropped all their pretenses and started singing songs straight. Rod Stewart had been a Jagger wannabe in his 1970s incarnation, and his voice was a postmodernist's dream, able to impart multiple levels of meaning, from the scurrilous to the supercilious, to any lyric. But in his late-career turnaround, Stewart embraced the same American pop song bag that Bennett had brought to MTV, digging deeply into the boy-meets-girl emotions of "I've Got a Crush on You" and "My Funny Valentine." The flippancy had disappeared from his interpretations, and the purposeful nature of Stewart's delivery was a revelation to those who'd known him only from "Maggie May" and "Da Ya Think I'm Sexy?" But this return to tradition proved to be a highly successful formula for Stewart, recharging his career and substantially boosting his record sales.

New artists today are following the same playbook, acting as though the last several decades of pop music had never taken place. Norah Jones grew up in Dallas listening to Billie Holiday while others of her generation were paying attention to the Spice Girls and Backstreet Boys. But her 2002 debut release, *Come Away with Me*, trumped all the boy bands and girl bands with its mix of standards and new songs that sounded like old ones, all performed the way Holiday did her songs—with her heart and soul on display. Jones's release was originally classified by industry trade journals as jazz—after all, pop music of this intimate sort was all but prohibited back in the midseventies—but by that measure Jones's single release accounted for 25 percent of the total industry jazz sales for the year. In fact, the recording spread like wildfire through the mainstream audience and would eventually sell a staggering twenty million copies worldwide. At the Grammy awards, Jones swept the four biggest awards: Record of the Year, Album of the Year, Song of the Year, and

Best New Artist—something that had not happened in more than twenty years. And she did all this by espousing musical values from the thirties!

Once attuned to this new earnestness in popular music, you hear it everywhere: in the soulful stylings of John Mayer; in Herbie Hancock's project (another surprise Grammy winner) based on the work of singer-songwriter Joni Mitchell; in the amazing posthumous success of singer Eva Cassidy, who became one of the biggest sellers of the new millennium despite passing away from melanoma in 1996; in Madeleine Peyroux's channeling of the spirit of Billie Holiday in contemporary pop form; in the vibrant new folk and acoustic scenes. Above all, you see it in the intensely unironic performances on *American Idol*, where sweet-as-pie and down-home are the qualities that win the day.

The same reversal is equally apparent in the world of classical music, where the coy performance-art games of the avant-garde have been displaced by a whole generation of composers who are dead serious about their art and are not ashamed to try for the most profound emotional (and even spiritual) effects. At first, the music of Henryk Górecki or Arvo Pärt struck listeners as anachronistic, a strange throwback to medieval times. Yet the audience seemed to crave just this sort of thing, buying up the recordings of these new medievalists with the same passion that they were also snatching up discs of Gregorian chant and Pachelbel's Canon. Other composers— Morton Lauridsen in the United States, John Tavener in Britain, Vladimír Godár in Slovakia—also found enthusiastic responses to the sobriety and seriousness in their music. Hostile critics have tried to explain this music away or wait quietly for it to give way to more deconstructive attacks on the audience's sensibilities. Reactionary movements (and in their minds, the renunciation of cool is a reactionary movement) always falter, they believe, and the progressives triumph in the end. But they have been waiting for quite some time, and no rescue party has yet arrived on the scene. Nor will it arrive soon, since these musical developments are not haphazard events, but are very much aligned with the new earnestness sweeping all aspects of contemporary culture in our postcool age.

In short, irony is on the ropes and is about to relinquish its long-held crown to the leaner and hungrier challengers waiting in the wings who are not so world-weary, not so jaded. Media companies are struggling to adapt to the new climate, replacing irony- and sarcasm-drenched sitcoms with reality shows, or trying to stake out ground with the real reality shows on YouTube and MySpace. Authenticity is hot right now, hotter than anything else. But the entertainment industry will not have an easy time co-opting this new trend—even when they try to be authentic, they do it with such phoniness and artifice that the magic disappears the moment they put their hands on it. Like New Age and Norah Jones, these return-to-the-basics movements invariably spring from places where multinational corporations have never looked.

No, YouTube is not the answer. No, *American Idol* is not the solution. But something has changed. The ironic age is quietly coming to an end. The new earnestness is upon us. We can sing the old songs again, sing them with feeling and not be embarrassed by it. But, even better, the new songs are also coming, and though I don't know exactly what they will sound like, I can already tell that they will come straight from the heart.

The Postcool Society

In 1992, Dave Ramsey was selling books out of the trunk of his car and spreading word of a new approach to personal finance he called *Financial Peace*. But who would want to take advice on money matters from someone who had recently declared bankruptcy? And even stranger was Ramsey's advice, which celebrated the joys of downscaling, eating rice and beans, and trading in the fancy car for a beat-up, used junker, all mixed in with a judicious dose of biblical teachings, traditional values, and free-market philosophizing. Even among the uncool, Ramsey was an extremist.

Ramsey hooked up with a bankrupt radio station, WWTN in Manchester, Tennessee, on the dubious premise that two broke and bankrupt parties made an even better platform for giving financial advice. WWTN had no money to pay Ramsey—so he did a show for free. His unusual message, which ran counter to almost everything else on the airwaves, found a surprisingly enthusiastic response. Soon Ramsey was one of the most popular radio hosts in the region, and WWTN not only emerged from bankruptcy, but became the highest-billing radio broadcaster in the Nashville market.

National syndicators were now coming to Ramsey's door, offering to put him on the air across the country. Ramsey refused to deal with these middlemen, but this did little to hinder his success. Despite his strange formula for his own personal financial peace—going bankrupt, working for free, turning down big money from syndicators, and so forth—his show was eventually picked up by more than four hundred radio stations, and he is one of the most successful self-syndicated talk-show hosts in the history of radio. Ramsey's downloadable shows consistently rank among the most popular podcasts on iTunes. He supplements his income through seminars, which are packed and take on the fervor of a revival meeting, and a series of best-selling books. In 2007, the Fox Business Network put Ramsey on cable television, where he continues to spread his philosophy of anticonsumerism, antistatus lifestyles, tithing, and downsizing.

In the cooler-than-cool and consumption-oriented eighties, a figure like Ramsey would have been a joke, a skit on *Saturday Night Live*. But today he is typical of the new tone and one of the propagators of the postcool worldview that is continually finding more and more adherents. And here is the strangest part of the story: Ramsey's views are surprisingly similar to those of opinion leaders at the opposite end of the ideological spectrum. We find a congruent message coming from leading left-wing antiglobalist Naomi Klein, who lashes out against corporations and the establishment in her book *No Logo*; or self-proclaimed culture jammer Kalle Lasn, who is also honing an anticonsumerism message that, if put into practice, would lead to a "lifestyle" not much different from that advocated by Ramsey's *Financial Peace*.

"Plenitude is American culture's perverse burden," Lasn writes.

> Most Americans have everything they could possibly want and they still don't think it's nearly enough. When everything is at hand, nothing is ever hard-won, and when nothing is ever hard-won, nothing really satisfies. In this era of gigantism—corporate megamergers, billion-dollar-grossing films and grande lattes— we embrace the value of More to compensate for lives that seem, somehow, less.[1]

When both sides of the culture wars espouse similar criticisms of contemporary society, something strange is afoot. But the most striking thing about the anticool movement is not the ideologues and intellectuals, but everyday people who don't write books or host radio and television shows. There have always been ascetics and hermits who renounced the ways of the world, who exempted themselves from conventional notions of status and affluence. But now these are increasingly the more influential and successful people in our communities. As we have already seen, statistics validate the existence of the millionaires next door whose external lifestyles run counter to every stereotyped view of affluence. A host of other lifestyles—back to nature, holistic, New Age, and the like—feed into these same attitudes and behavior patterns. Not too long ago, these attitudes existed only on the fringe, in out-of-the-way communes or tiny pockets of counterculture rebels. Now they have shown up on Main Street. For a growing number of individuals, the traditional trappings of coolness, wealth, and a fashionable image are renounced as unnecessary or, even more, as frivolous and immature.

Although both sides of the culture war will try to co-opt this issue for their own purposes—and have already started to do so—the decooling of society won't be the property of any single political agenda or ideological combatant. The shift is taking place at a deeper psychological level, and though it will feed activism and political campaigns and social movements, it cannot be reduced to a series of op-ed talking points. This deep-seated ambivalence, and sometimes out-and-out distaste, for the cool, is much like the resistance biological organisms develop after they have been exposed repeatedly to the same stimuli. The stimulus loses its effectiveness and in time may produce an actual aversion. The dominance of cool has reached a saturation point over the last decade, and a larger and larger portion of the public no longer responds to the message. Cool is increasingly just cultural noise, and people have developed a variety of tools to block it out.

In his book *American Cool: Constructing a Twentieth-Century Emotional Style*, Peter N. Stearns describes how the cool attitude was itself a reaction to rigid Victorian attitudes and behavior patterns. "The Victorian middle class used its emotional culture to help differentiate itself from other groups, particularly working-class immigrants," Stearns writes.[2] These entrenched behavior patterns reflected a judgmental society, which was quick to exclude, to show its disdain or even anger—often as a barely disguised way of enforcing class privileges. Yet by the fifties, when the cool took off, this attempt at elitism no longer had much value for the typical young American. By the midcentury mark, the vast majority of Americans saw themselves as middle class and part of the mainstream of society. For the new generation coming of age then, standing out from the crowd now meant avoiding at all costs the mind-numbing middle-class values and pseudo-Victorian attitudes that had come to permeate all of American life. To achieve this, trendsetters looked to precisely those groups that had been excluded or viewed with suspicion by their parents' generation—blacks, gays, jazz musicians, street toughs, bohemians, and counterculture figures of all stripes—as the new role models.

The vibrancy of this new cool attitude was intoxicating—at least for a time. And even after it had lost its novelty, it still retained a certain residual momentum that kept it in ascendancy for several decades. But the very success with which cool took over the mass market and middle class resulted in the loss of its piquancy. Any dish that you consume over and over again tends to do that.

An ennui and sense of exhaustion set in and only became more pronounced as the merchants of cool redoubled their efforts. Even more to the point, the cool abandoned its emotional and psychological supports once it shifted from being a charismatic force residing in people and became reified as an attribute of merchandise. Cool's original power had derived from its formative role in forging a modern personality type, a style of engagement—indirect, ironic, flexible, infused with humor, sometimes flippant—that was adopted with success by a growing percentage of the population. But the relentless mass marketing of cool has tainted this style of behavior and made it seem inauthentic or contrived to a growing number of individuals. It is almost inconceivable that anything could happen, at this late stage, that would restore to the cool the freshness and vitality it possessed in the fifties and sixties.

Of course, the old-school cool ethos will not disappear completely. Even when some color or fabric is passé, it still finds its way into our wardrobe. But cool now lacks conviction and energy. Above all, its economic force is diminishing. And this, more than anything, will accelerate its decline. One busy cash register is worth more than a thousand pundits. The arbiters of taste—at record labels, in film and TV, in consumer marketing, in media—will respond to these economic shifts rather than lead them. But follow they must, or disappear from the scene. Their successors will not make the same mistakes. Over time, this will transform even the last institutional bastions of cool into promoters of the postcool worldview.

One of the most interesting spectacles of postcool society will involve the dominant forces of the old paradigm scrambling to co-opt the new one. Packaged and slick and phony will attempt to become down-home and natural and authentic. We can see this playing out in many arenas—from music to clothing, politics to daily news. But let us take one sector of our economy and show how this works.

In consumer food products, the postcool celebration of the natural and authentic is spelled out in the recent dramatic growth in the sale of organic fruits and vegetables, vitamin supplements, antibiotic- and hormone-free beef, and other products that previously existed only on the fringes of the food industry. Of course, this trend spells trouble for packaged-food multinationals, who are the real losers here. How do they respond? In the postcool society, representatives of the old paradigm imitate the new one. So we have the Naked Juice company, with its line of 100 percent natural, unsweetened beverages...but it's owned by Pepsi. The registered slogan of this company is "Nothing to Hide"—but one thing is clearly hidden in its marketing campaigns: its connection with PepsiCo Inc.! (Visit the Naked Juice website, and see if you can find the name of the parent company anywhere. Good luck!) Then again, Naked Juice needs to deal with its competitor Odwalla, a leader in all-natural juices...which is owned by Coca-Cola.

Next stop on your itinerary, please visit the website for Dagoba, a company committed to the highest-quality organic chocolate, and see if you can find any mention of parent company Hershey. But Mars Inc., maker of M&Ms and Snickers, has gone even further, acquiring Seeds of Change, which sells more than six hundred types of 100 percent organically grown seeds. And we have the Back to Nature brand of cereal and granola...but it is now owned by Kraft Foods, makers of Cheez Whiz and Velveeta. Heinz, through its minority position in Hain Celestial, has an equity share in dozens of natural food brands. I could cite countless other examples. In fact, almost every major purveyor of packaged, processed food loaded with preservatives and various chemicals is trying to position itself as a champion of healthy, natural eating.

But the fascinating angle here is how well hidden these relationships are. In the old days, Hershey would make sure everyone knew they were involved when they sold chocolate. After all, what could be a better endorsement for confections than the Hershey brand name? Or Coca-Cola's for beverages? Or Pepsi's? These companies have invested billions of dollars in building and enhancing the value of their brand names. Pepsi alone has purchased celebrity endorsements at untold cost from Britney Spears, Mariah Carey, Pink, Christina Aguilera, Michael Jackson, Janet Jackson, David Beckham, David Bowie, Shakira, Jackie Chan, Halle Berry, Jennifer Lopez, Tina Turner, Justin Timberlake, Beyoncé Knowles, Mary J. Blige, the Spice Girls, Ray Charles, and many, many others. Yet now this company needs to conceal its involvement in the fastest-growing segments of the beverage market? What gives? We see the same odd shift in field after field—music, media, consumer products, retailing, politics, fashions, academics, the Internet, almost anywhere you look. Organizations that have spent decades investing in their image, their brand, their logo, now admit that it's best to junk all that and start with a clean sheet of paper.

This paradox will become a part of day-to-day life in the postcool society. Even if postcool celebrates the real and authentic, the simple and down to earth, it doesn't mean that these attributes will actually dominate public life. Instead, we will find a grand charade of phony pretending to be authentic, of contrived acting as though it is real, the intricately planned putting on the mask of the simple and unaffected. In many instances, postcool will just be the same folks who brought you cool, hiding behind a mask.

But this faux postcool will increasingly be forced to compete with the real thing. Grassroots movements will be built around the core postcool values of simplicity, authenticity, naturalness, and earnestness. These will flourish outside the marketplace, in public and private discourse, shaping attitudes and interpersonal relations. True, they will have an economic impact, but their significance will not be reducible to dollars and cents. Postcool will inhabit people's psyches long before it takes control of their wallets.

This core distinction will be our chief guide in distinguishing the phony corporate maneuverings from the real grassroots changes that will drive postcool society. The former will always inhabit a product or service. And if the cool was a friend to business, seeing its own destiny in accessories and gadgets, the postcool will have a more ambivalent relationship with the prevailing economic interests. The new ethos does not require expensive new accessories and often will take positive delight in downscaling lifestyles and paring back on unneeded extras.

Simplicity, authenticity, naturalness, and earnestness…I mentioned these as though they were parts of a product-positioning exercise. But in fact they will be the foundations of the postcool personality type. Just as the cool was at its best when internalized as a way people acted and not just trumpeted as a marketing message, so will postcool have its greatest impact as a way people instinctively deal with situations and circumstances. In a book such as this, the examples gathered inevitably come from things that can be seen, heard, touched, measured—in short, what we call empirical evidence. But don't let that fool you into thinking that these are the primary signs of the new postcool era. Many of the most salient changes will be those that we can grasp only indirectly and will not be measurable with any exactitude by statisticians and pollsters.

For this same reason, postcool will be less fickle and changeable than cool. Postcool is *not* just another style, another trend. It is the antithesis of style, of trendiness. And because it reflects an emerging personality type and not a passing fashion, postcool will probably be around for quite a while. Many merchants of cool will be tempted to dismiss or misinterpret postcool, seeing its key elements as a new, marketable lifestyle, as just one more way of being cool. We can already see many examples of this shortsighted behavior. But ultimately the attempt to treat postcool as just another variant on the cool will fail.

For fifty years, the prevailing tone has been focused outward. Cool was in the eyes of the beholder, and those who lived by its principles needed constantly to be attuned to what others were thinking and doing. As trends and fashions and languages changed, the cool cats had to change as well…or risk being left behind. And even though good guys are expected to finish last, according to the adage, cool cats are not allowed to bring up the rear. The cool was a demanding deity, requiring its adherents to keep up with the times, to maintain a retinue of admirers. But postcool, by nature inward focused and self-directed, will not be so easily budged. From now on, the game will be played by different rules.

Postcool will be more intense than cool. Higher strung. More determined and less easily deflected and distracted. For this reason, many parties will strive to win the allegiance of this rapidly growing constituency. Political candidates will build their campaigns to appeal to the new psyche. Marketers will position products to maximize their perceived value to this demographic. Social movements and churches and media will all try to attract them. Who wouldn't want these assertive, strong-willed folks in their camp? But the challenges involved in securing their support should not be minimized. The postcool person is not a belonger, not a follower. As Arnold Mitchell discovered when he first identified this group in the seventies—when it was just a tiny subset of the American public, maybe 1 or 2 percent by his measure—these individuals are the hardest to market to…because by their nature they are suspicious of marketing and resistant to its methods.

As a result, the postcool society will be full of surprises. The scene will be marked by unexpected grassroots activities that come to the fore *despite* the best-laid plans of politicians and corporate execs. Exciting? Perhaps. Dangerous and volatile? Certainly at times.

Of course, even postcool may sow the seeds of its own eventual decline. A new personality type lasts longer than a passing fashion, but even deep-seated character patterns and emotional styles can outlive their usefulness. Just as the cool personality became less effective over time, postcool could find itself replaced by some yet-to-be-defined paradigm. We can already see postcool's vulnerability in its unstable reliance on bluntness and aggression, its susceptibility to anger and confrontation. When so much irritability and adversarial posturing permeate our national and local lives, won't this breed another reaction in time, a new cooling down of the temperature and the reemergence of consensus building and a softer, gentler emotional style in public and private life?

But old-school cool will not come back. The cool is dead…at least as we knew it back in the second half of the twentieth century. If aspects of it still hold center stage from time to time, they will do so because they have adapted to the new state of affairs. As with all passing movements, the Age of Cool will inspire nostalgia and retain a few adherents, those folks who always look back dreamily at the past, lamenting the loss of the good ol' days. But the future belongs to a different personality type, marked by earnestness, sincerity, skepticism, simplicity, and hard-nosed assertiveness. It's like everything Mom and Dad told you is finally coming true…only now you will be hearing it from your own children.

So close the book on twentieth-century cool. It was a wild and fun ride while it lasted. When historians look back, they may see it as the pinnacle of what people are already calling the American Century. As economic power shifts to the rapidly growing economies of Asia, something of the practicality and industriousness of those developing countries will permeate Western ways. In truth, they may be the exemplars of the new postcool mandate. In any event, a different tone has emerged, and we now must let it run its course—for better or worse. Even so, I can't help feeling more than a twinge of regret. No, the cool folks won't inherit the earth. But they certainly showed us a good time while they were around.

The Birth {and Death} of the Cool: A Timeline

1885

Sunglasses first developed to serve as protective eyewear for reducing the glare of snowy terrain.

1886

Cosmopolitan begins publishing in New York.

The gas-fueled automobile is invented.

Avon is founded as the California Perfume Company by door-to-door salesman David H. McConnell.

1888

Antiperspirant is invented, establishing cool as a matter of personal hygiene.

1890

Levi Strauss introduces the original 501 blue jeans. In 2005, a Japanese collector pays $60,000 in an eBay auction for a pair.

1891

Rayon, the first artificial fiber to be commercialized, is produced in France. The material is marketed as a soft, smooth, cool, and comfortable alternative to natural fibers.

1892

Sears Roebuck sends out a mass mailing of eight thousand postcards with imitation handwriting to mimic a personal letter. Spam is born, but more than two thousand orders result from this corporate deception.

Vogue magazine is founded by Arthur Baldwin Turnure.

1899

Scott Joplin publishes "The Maple Leaf Rag," which becomes the first instrumental piece of sheet music to sell more than one million copies—bringing a taste of black culture into the parlors of mainstream America.

1903

In Dahomey, the first all–African American musical production, comes to Broadway.

1906

The First Annual Advertising Show opens in New York. The age of branding begins.

1918

Humphrey Bogart is expelled from Phillips Academy and never makes it (as his parents had hoped) to Yale. Possible reasons for his dismissal include smoking, drinking, rude language, and an intemperate outburst—all of which he will adopt in perfecting his persona as the ultimate Hollywood antihero.

1919

Swiss conductor Ernst-Alexandre Ansermet predicts that American jazz will be "the highway the whole world will swing along tomorrow."

1921

The first Miss America pageant is held in Atlantic City, New Jersey.

Gabrielle "Coco" Chanel rejects the perfumes in the bottles marked 1 through 4, as well as number 6. But Chanel No. 5 gets the green light and is launched. In 1953, when Marilyn Monroe is asked what she wears to bed, she replies, "Two drops of Chanel No. 5."

1923

Converse puts Chuck Taylor's signature on its All-Star shoe—and goes on to sell more than 750 million pairs.

1927

Bix Beiderbecke and Frank Trumbauer record "Singin' the Blues," a prototype of cool jazz, although the term itself will not appear until more than two decades have elapsed.

The car radio is introduced. Consumers can now bring their personal soundtrack with them on the road.

1928

The clip-on tie is invented.

1929

A translation of Alfred Adler's *Problems of Neurosis* introduces the term *lifestyle* into the English vocabulary.

Sunglasses come to the beach when Sam Foster begins selling them on the Atlantic City Boardwalk.

1930

Babe Ruth becomes the first sports star to make more than the president of the United States. When asked to justify this discrepancy, the ballplayer replies, "I had a better year than he [Herbert Hoover] did."

1931

Casino gambling legalized in Nevada.

1932

A scholar writing in the journal *American Speech* notes that "jazz slang" is slipping into conversational English through its incorporation in the lyrics of popular songs.

1933

Fluorescent colors invented.

The first drive-in movie theater opens in Pennsauken, New Jersey.

1934

Clark Gable scorns the use of undershirts in the film *It Happened One Night.*

Chrysler launches the Airflow, the first mass-marketed streamlined car.

1936

Saxophonist Lester Young makes his first recording with Count Basie. In later years, Basie bandmates will insist that Young was the first to use the term *cool* with its modern significance of hipness.

Billboard magazine launches its popular music chart.

The first drive-in restaurant opens in Glendale, California.

1937

Ray-Ban introduces Aviator sunglasses.

1938

Cab Calloway publishes his *Cat-ologue: A Hepsters Dictionary,* but does not include the term *cool.*

1940

Nylon stockings launched nationwide.

Bugs Bunny first asks, "What's up, Doc?" The cartoon character adopts a wide range of cool mannerisms a decade before they become common in public life.

1943

Woody Brown and Dickie Cross try to catch fifty-foot waves at Waimea Bay—then untouched by surfers. Brown survives, washing ashore, but Cross never returns.

Frank Sinatra becomes the first pop singer to find himself besieged by screaming female fans.

1944

Dan Burley publishes his *Original Handbook of Harlem Jive* and mentions *cool* in passing, but does not include a definition in his lexicon.

Seventeen magazine is launched and sells 400,000 copies in less than a week.

Pharmacist Benjamin Green invents Coppertone suntan cream in his kitchen. He proves its efficacy by testing it on his bald head.

1946

The bikini is introduced. Five years later, the bikini is banned from the Miss World contest following the crowning of Miss Sweden, who adopts the fabric-conserving fashion for the swimsuit competition.

1947

Polaroid launches the Land Camera, making instant photography widely available.

1948

The transistor radio is invented.

Alfred Kinsey publishes *Sexual Behavior in the Human Male*.

Detroit introduces air-conditioning in cars—contemporary cool entering the American automobile at roughly the same time it enters the American lexicon.

1949

Miles Davis makes his first cool jazz studio recordings. These sell poorly at the time, but are far more successful when reissued in 1954 under the name *Birth of the Cool*.

Lee Strasberg begins teaching at The Actors Studio, where he mentors many of the fifties movie stars who will bring the cool ethos to the silver screen.

1950

Hollywood makes its first big-budget jazz bio flick, *Young Man with a Horn*, loosely based on the life of Bix Beiderbecke.

Dr. Seuss introduces the word *nerd* in his book *If I Ran the Zoo*. The usage and meaning of the word will expand in tandem with the cool ethos, typically signifying its opposite.

Diners Club card is introduced as the first status-oriented charge card.

1951

J. D. Salinger publishes *The Catcher in the Rye*.

Miss World beauty pageant founded.

1952

Miss Universe and Miss USA beauty pageants founded.

Ray-Ban introduces Wayfarer sunglasses.

After participating on the *Birth of the Cool* sessions, saxophonist Gerry Mulligan hitchhikes to California, where he is influential in establishing the West Coast jazz movement.

1953

"What're you rebelling against?" Marlon Brando is asked in the film *The Wild One*. He replies, "Whaddya got?"

Sales of black leather jackets take off in response to Brando's adoption of the fashion in *The Wild One*.

1954

Steve Allen serves as host for the first broadcast of *The Tonight Show*.

1955

Helena Rubinstein launches a new lipstick-brand jazz, with the slogan "Red, Hot—and Cool!"

Miles Davis stirs up the crowd at the Newport Jazz Festival with his ballad performance of "'Round Midnight." As a result of this unanticipated success, Davis is signed by the Columbia label.

Hollywood tries to make jazz trumpeter Chet Baker into a movie star, casting him in the forgettable *Hell's Horizon*.

James Dean appears in *Rebel Without a Cause*.

Sixty percent of Americans are now classified as "middle class" (defined at the time as having income between $3,000 and $10,000 per year).

1956

City Lights Bookstore publishes Allen Ginsberg's *Howl*.

Arnold Neustadter of Brooklyn, New York, patents the Rolodex. The age of networking begins.

More than sixty million Americans see Elvis Presley (mostly from the waist up) on *The Ed Sullivan Show*.

1957

Norman Mailer proclaims that "the source of hip is the Negro" in his influential and often ridiculed essay "The White Negro."

Viking Press publishes Jack Kerouac's novel *On the Road*.

Seven intrepid surfers are the first to successfully ride the massive waves at Waimea Bay.

1958

Invention of the skateboard.

Television now reaches 83 percent of American households, only one decade after the commercialization of this technology.

San Francisco Chronicle columnist Herb Caen coins the term *beatnik*.

1959

Motown Records founded in Detroit.

John Severson publishes the first surf magazine, called *Surfer*.

1960

The first Playboy Club opens its doors in Chicago. Before the close of the decade, membership will reach 750,000.

Warner Bros. releases the classic Rat Pack movie *Ocean's Eleven*, featuring Frank Sinatra, Dean Martin, Sammy Davis Jr., and Peter Lawford.

John F. Kennedy defeats Richard Nixon in a close presidential race, and many commentators attribute the margin of victory to Kennedy's more polished media image on the candidates' televised debates. Nixon, classically uncool, perspires heavily.

1962

Sean Connery stars in the first James Bond movie, *Dr. No*.

Lycra launched by DuPont and touted for its "comfort, fit, and freedom of movement."

1963

American International Pictures releases *Beach Party*, the first major beach movie, and follows up the next year with *Muscle Beach Party*.

Harvey Ball develops Smiley, the happy-face graphic popularized in the seventies on T-shirts, coffee mugs, bumper stickers, and other merchandise.

1964

Seventy-three million people watch The Beatles on *The Ed Sullivan Show.*

Ford introduces the Mustang and sells more then one million cars during the first eighteen months.

Goldfinger is a box office blockbuster and becomes the fastest-grossing film of all time. Sean Connery (playing James Bond) drives a gadget-laded Aston Martin DB5 and specifies that his martinis should be "shaken, not stirred."

1965

CBS scores a fifty-share hit with *A Charlie Brown Christmas,* despite predictions that it would fail due to the absence of a laugh track and its unconventional cool jazz soundtrack.

Miniskirts become the latest fashion craze. Model Jean Shrimpton shocks onlookers at the Victoria Derby race by wearing a white shift dress that ended 3.9 inches above her knees.

When asked what might tempt him to sell out, Bob Dylan comments, "Ladies' undergarments." (Fast-forward: In 2004, Bob Dylan signs a deal allowing Victoria's Secret to use his song "Love Sick" in an ad campaign.)

Bell-bottoms, formerly worn by sailors, become the latest fashion craze.

1966

John Lennon claims that The Beatles are "bigger than Jesus."

1967

The first issue of *Rolling Stone* magazine is published by Jann Wenner and Ralph J. Gleason.

"Sometimes nothin' can be a real cool hand," Paul Newman announces in the film *Cool Hand Luke*.

1969

A half million people attend the Woodstock Festival.

The Concorde, the stylish supersonic passenger jet, makes its first flight.

1970

The waterbed, first envisioned by sci-fi writer Robert Heinlein, is commercialized.

1974

People magazine is launched as a spin-off of the "People" page in *Time* magazine.

1975

Gary Dahl becomes a millionaire by selling Pet Rocks.

1976

The first Harlequin Romance is published.

Neal Frost coins the term *elevator music*.

1977

Arnold Mitchell and Duane Elgin publish their report "Voluntary Simplicity," predicting the rise of a large group of individuals who will deliberately choose lifestyles that renounce consumption and traditional measures of status.

1978

Blue Ribbon Sports, founded in 1964 by Bill Bowerman and Philip Knight, changes its name to Nike.

Brian Eno releases his *Ambient 1: Music for Airports.*

1980

Ray-Ban Wayfarer sunglasses become cool again after they are featured in the movie *The Blues Brothers.*

The Official Preppy Handbook becomes a surprise best seller.

The first Whole Foods Market opens in Austin, Texas.

Dan Rottenberg introduces the term *yuppie*—an abbreviation for "young upwardly mobile professionals" (or "young urban professionals"), a group that includes many of the same people who were branded as hippies a few years before.

1981

MTV is launched, with a format initially devoted to music videos.

1982

Former radical activist Jerry Rubin opens Jerry Rubin's Business Networking Salon in New York, where he promotes social events organized for the purpose of networking.

Jane Fonda releases her first workout video.

1983

Sales of Ray-Ban Wayfarers are given another boost after Tom Cruise dons them for his role in *Risky Business.*

1984

Nike signs Michael Jordan to a five-year $2.5-million endorsement deal.

Arnold Mitchell of SRI publishes *The Nine American Lifestyles,* a landmark event in the corporatization of the cool. This work legitimizes lifestyle marketing and the matching of product concepts to psychographic profiles.

Warning sign Baby on Board becomes popular on cars.

1986

Clint Eastwood is elected mayor of Carmel, California.

Levi Strauss introduces Dockers casual slacks. Dave Barry will later describe their target market in succinct terms: they are "pants for the bigger-butted man."

Huey Lewis and The News release the single "It's Hip to Be Square," which reaches number three on the *Billboard* Hot 100.

1987

Nike uses The Beatles' song "Revolution" in a controversial commercial that is savagely attacked as a sellout by rock fans.

Southern California radio station KTWV launches "The Wave," promoting a successful format initially known as "new adult contemporary" but eventually dubbed "smooth jazz."

1988

Gap launches its Individuals of Style campaign, featuring black-and-white photographs of celebrities wearing Gap products.

The last Playboy Club shuts its doors in Lansing, Michigan.

The Music Institute, an influential club featuring techno music, opens in Detroit.

1989

Fifteen-year-old Michael Eugene Thomas is strangled by a classmate who wants his $115 pair of Air Jordans.

1991

Miles Davis dies at age sixty-five. In his later recordings, he renounced the cool aesthetic that brought him to fame in the fifties.

1992

Bill Clinton appears on *The Arsenio Hall Show* wearing shades and playing the saxophone.

Kenny G's smooth jazz CD *Breathless* establishes smooth jazz as a major commercial style. Despite being savaged by jazz critics, this recording becomes the biggest-selling instrumental CD of all time.

MTV launches *The Real World*, giving birth to the reality show genre.

Richard Majors and Janet Mancini Billson publish *Cool Pose: The Dilemmas of Black Manhood in America.*

Adbusters magazine promotes the first "Buy Nothing Day" to focus public attention on overconsumption. In later years, this annual event is promoted by groups in some sixty-five countries.

1993

Apple Computer launches the Newton personal digital assistant. The product is a flop, but from now on the words *cool* and *gadget* will go hand in hand.

Jack Kerouac, dead since 1969, is featured in an ad for khakis by Gap.

Wired magazine is launched and proves that it is possible to cover technology with the glitz and image orientation that *Vogue* brings to fashion. No one is surprised when, in 2006, Condé Nast—the publisher of *Vogue*—acquires *Wired*.

The term *going postal*—to describe a violent workplace outburst by a disgruntled employee—first appears in print (in the *St. Petersburg Times*).

1994

Gap launches the Old Navy brand and opens fifty-seven stores during the first year. The retailing concept is targeted at consumers who are more price-sensitive than the typical Gap demographic.

Sonny Bono is elected to Congress.

Hot confronts cool when Tonya Harding is linked to an attack on her skating rival, Nancy Kerrigan. Kerrigan nonetheless recovers and wins a silver medal at the Winter Olympics.

Frank Sinatra gives his final public concert in Japan.

The CD reissue of an old recording of Gregorian chants, *Chant*, released by the Benedictine Monks of Santo Domingo de Silos, sells five million copies.

1995

Microsoft secures permission from the Rolling Stones to use their song "Start Me Up" for the launch of its Windows 95 operating system.

Michael Jordan signs an endorsement deal with Rayovac batteries.

IBM softens its totalitarian dress code, allowing casual attire for the first time.

Mercedes-Benz first uses Janis Joplin's song "Mercedes Benz"—originally recorded as a satirical commentary on materialist consumption—in a commercial touting its automobiles.

1996

Palm launches the first Palm Pilot.

Walmart begins using Smiley, the happy-face symbol popularized during the seventies, on uniforms, signs, and promotional materials.

Nike signs a $40-million endorsement deal with Tiger Woods. Woods also signs with Titleist for $20 million.

Harvard Business School receives 8,050 applications for the class of '98—a sharp increase from 6,970 the previous year, and up threefold compared with 1966.

Comedian Eddie Murphy abandons his street-smart hip persona and reinvents himself in *The Nutty Professor*. He follows up with *Dr. Dolittle*, *Daddy Day Care*, and a host of very uncool but financially lucrative projects.

1997

Malcolm Gladwell writes "The Coolhunt" for *The New Yorker*, the most influential of a now-growing number of guides that show how corporations can co-opt coolness.

1998

The Bugatti brand name is acquired by Volkswagen.

Nike is sued over sweatshop conditions. The company's stock falls to $31 from the previous-year high of $76.

1999

General Motors signs Tiger Woods to endorse its Buick line. The average age of a Buick owner is sixty-five.

Google founders Larry Page and Sergey Brin enlist Ruth Kedar to design their logo. Their goal is that "Google as a brand should repudiate all things corporate, conventional, or complacent."

Anticorporate activist Kalle Lasn publishes his book *Culture Jam: The Uncooling of America*. Lasn defines *culture jammer* as someone who "disrupts the status quo of corporate influence."

2000

Journalist and activist Naomi Klein publishes *No Logo*.

MTV, which once played music videos 24/7, now only broadcasts an average of eight hours of music videos per day.

Real Simple magazine launched.

2001

Talk magazine folds after burning through $50 million in funding.

Novelist Fay Weldon is criticized after receiving £18,000 from the jeweler Bulgari in exchange for name placement in her novel *The Bulgari Connection*.

Sales of SUVs, minivans, and pickups surpass car sales for the first time.

Apple launches the first iPod. Over the next six years, the company will sell more than 150 million units.

2002

Sony Ericsson's use of paid shills to promote its T68i cell phone is publicized by *The Wall Street Journal*.

American Idol debuts on the Fox network.

Come Away with Me, a recording of underproduced love songs by previously unknown singer Norah Jones, is a surprise hit and goes on to sell twenty million copies.

2003

Nike signs LeBron James to a $90-million multiyear endorsement deal.

Millions of youngsters purchase and read a 255,000-word novel called *Harry Potter and the Order of the Phoenix*. More than 200 million copies of the previous books in the Harry Potter series have been sold, and translations have brought the story into fifty-five languages.

The Concorde, the stylish supersonic passenger jet, makes its last commercial flight.

MySpace is launched. Almost exactly three years later, the 100 millionth MySpace account is opened.

2004

Facebook is launched. Over the next four years, it attracts 100 million users.

ABC drops coverage of the Miss America beauty pageant after its broadcast of the event attracts fewer than ten million viewers.

Forbes announces that James Dean has more than fifty endorsement deals, despite being dead for almost fifty years.

2005

Transitions Optical Inc. shifts the marketing emphasis on the company's photochromic sunglasses from fashionability to health benefits and the need to block UV rays.

2006

The Federal Trade Commission steps in to regulate the manipulation of word-of-mouth marketing.

Gray-haired Taylor Hicks from Birmingham, Alabama, beats out sultry So Cal singer Katherine McPhee in the *American Idol* finals—with more than 63 million votes tabulated.

Real Simple launches its PBS television show.

Los Angeles Times reports that video blogger lonelygirl15 is actually a front for California filmmakers posing as a sixteen-year-old girl in order to generate word-of-mouth marketing for their work.

The magazine *Fast Company* reports that many companies are "outsourcing cool."

2007

Hacker Virgil Griffith launches WikiScanner—a Web-based tool that allows people to identify businesses and organizations that are making anonymous changes to their own Wikipedia entries.

Sales of Pokémon games surpass 150 million.

Starbucks announces that it will ramp up television advertising to strengthen its brand. Over the next six months, Starbucks stock falls by more than 30 percent.

Apple launches the iPhone.

The Big Bang Theory and *Chuck* debut on the same day and join the growing number of TV shows (*Ugly Betty*, *Beauty and the Geek*, etc.) celebrating the joys of nerdiness.

Dave Ramsey, the guru of downscaling, launches a TV show on the Fox Business Network.

2008

Marié Digby's debut CD flops after the media reports that her image as a self-produced artist was orchestrated by Hollywood Records, a subsidiary of the Walt Disney Company.

MTV, which once featured music videos round the clock, continues to shift its emphasis to reality shows and now broadcasts only three hours of music videos per day.

Nike discloses in its financial reports that its endorsement and sponsorship obligations surpass $3 billion for the first time—and have tripled since 2002.

2009

Unprepossessing Susan Boyle becomes a hit on *Britain's Got Talent*, and within nine days of her TV appearance her video performance of "Cry Me a River" is viewed more than 100 million times on the Internet.

General Motors announces that it will discontinue its Pontiac brand, which helped define the so-called muscle cars of the 1960s and reached peak sales back in 1973.

India's Tata Motors creates the automobile sensation of the year—not with the Jaguar brand it recently purchased from Ford, but with its $2,000 Nano car, which sells out its complete production run even before its official launch date.

Social networking website Twitter grows site traffic from under 500,000 visitors to more than seven million during a period of twelve months—a stunning increase of 1,382 percent. Early in the year, it surpasses the BBC and *The New York Times* as a popular Web destination.

Notes

1 Can Cool Ever Be Uncool?

1. See http://uncoolbook.blogspot.com/2007/02/revolutionaryjesus.html.
2. Gorlick, "'Integrity' Tops Web Dictionary's Lookups."
3. Robinson, "The Return of the Media Queen."
4. Carr, "Don't Aspire, Just Embrace Simplicity, Magazines Say."
5. Quotes from Conan O'Brien, Jenna Fischer, and Lorne Michaels from Windolf, "What's Funny Now?" 41–43.
6. Cottle, "The Cool Presidency," 14–16.
7. Turow, "When He Was Seventeen," 1, 10.
8. Thorn, "Finders Keepers," May 21, 2005.
9. Smith and Lattman, "Download This," A1.
10. Shin, "FTC Moves to Unmask Word-of-Mouth Marketing," D1.
11. Upshaw, *Truth: The New Rules for Marketing in a Skeptical World*, 2.
12. Lewis and Bridger, *The Soul of the New Consumer*, 3.

2 The Mystery of My Parents' Lifestyle

1. Nunberg, "The Evolution of 'Lifestyle.'"
2. McLuhan, "The Southern Quality," 357–383.
3. Reich, *The Greening of America*, 241.
4. Ibid., 239.
5. Cooper, Stern, and Mitchell, *Consumer Values and Demand*.
6. Mitchell, *The Nine American Lifestyles*, viii.
7. Guns, interview with author, March 17, 2008.
8. This is a thumbnail summary of the original VALS categories. For more details, see Mitchell, *The Nine American Lifestyles*, 61–149.
9. Ibid., 154.
10. Doherty and Etzioni, *Voluntary Simplicity*, 146.
11. Brinkley, "Inside a Salon That Serves the Logo-Phobic," D-8.
12. Keen, "Economic Survivalists Take Root."
13. Noonan, "Goodbye Bland Affluence," A13.
14. Nunberg, "The Evolution of 'Lifestyle.'"

3 How Cool Became So

1. Zhong and Leonardelli. "Cold and Lonely," 838–842.
2. For this and below, see *cool* in *The Random House Dictionary of American Slang*, 474–475. I am also indebted to Jesse Sheidlower of Oxford University Press, truly a man of many words in his capacity as editor-at-large with the *Oxford English Dictionary*, for his advice on the changing meaning of the word *cool*.
3. *The Slim Gaillard Vout-o-Reenee Dictionary*, an undated booklet, is often referred to as dating from the 1930s, but from the ads in its advertising records from 1945 touting it as a "new release," we should probably assume a mid-1940s release date.
4. Southgate, "Coolhunting with Aristotle," 167–190.
5. Thompson, "An Aesthetic of Cool," 40–43, 64–67, 89–91.
6. Castiglione, *The Book of the Courtier*, 43. See also Gioia, *West Coast Jazz*, 245, where I was the first to dub Castiglione as "father of the cool"—my sole contribution to the field of Renaissance studies.
7. Gates, *The Signifying Monkey*, 54.
8. Ibid., 6.
9. Ibid., 66.
10. Alexander, "Cool Like Me," 51–53.

4 The Progenitor of Cool: Bix Beiderbecke

1. Ansermet, "Bechet & Jazz Visit Europe, 1919," 115–122.
2. Sudhalter, *Lost Chords*, 29.
3. Lion, *Bix: The Definitive Biography*, 29.
4. Freeman and Wolf, *Crazeology*, 11.
5. Hilbert, *Pee Wee Russell*, 44.
6. This and below from Berton, *Remembering Bix*, xii.
7. Condon, *We Called It Music*, 121.
8. Mezzrow and Wolfe, *Really the Blues*, 79.
9. Ibid., 79.
10. Manone and Vandervoort, *Trumpet on the Wing*, 60.
11. Berton, *Remembering Bix*, 401.
12. Sudhalter, Evans, and Dean-Myatt, *Bix: Man and Legend*, 185.
13. Giddins and Schoenberg, "Jazz Dialogue."

5 The President of Cool: Lester Young

1. This comment from Jimmy Rowles and the John Lewis quote that follows from Balliett, *American Musicians*, 237–238.
2. For some of the usages and other examples, see Bryan Koniarz, "A Hipster's Dictionary," included in the accompanying booklet to *The Complete Lester Young Studio Sessions on Verve*, 35–38.
3. This story has been recounted in many settings, and I heard it directly from Stan Getz, who is its original source. It can be traced back in its expurgated form (with Sonny Stitt's name removed) to Don DeMichael," A Long Look at Stan Getz," *Downbeat*, May 19, 1966, 19.
4. Phil Schaap, e-mail message to author, April 8, 2008.
5. Büchmann-Møller, *You Just Fight for Your Life*, 121–122.

6 The Prince of Darkness: Miles Davis

1. Davis and Troupe, *Miles*, 45.
2. Ibid., 52.
3. Ibid., 148.

7 The Signifying Bunny, Or the Birth (and Death) of the Cool for Kids

1. Gates, *The Signifying Monkey*, 54.
2. St. John, "Seriously, the Joke Is Dead," ST 1 and 2.
3. Majors and Billson, *Cool Pose*, 1.
4. Bostrom, *The 21st Century Teen*, 6.
5. Penn and Zalesne, *Microtrends*, 167–169.
6. Francomano, Lavitt, and Lavitt, *Junior Achievement*, 94.
7. The information here comes from the following Junior Achievement press releases: "87 Percent of Youth Feel Prepared to Enter Workforce According to JA Worldwide Poll" (February 6, 2007); "Nine Out of Ten Students Believe College Will Help Them Start a Business" (August 28, 2006); "New JA/Deloitte Poll Indicates Teens Have Strong Ethical Compass" (September 20, 2005); "Teens Feel Intense Pressure to Succeed—According to JA/Deloitte Poll" (December 6, 2006); "Parents and Teachers Top Role Models for Second Year in a Row" (March 8, 2004).

8 Everybody Acts Like Miles Davis

1. This and below from O'Neil, "The Only Rebellion Around," 114–130.
2. Brady, "The New Cult of Sex and Anarchy," 312–322.
3. Broyard, "A Portrait of a Hipster," 721–728.
4. See for example Kerouac, "The Last Word," 72, and Kerouac, "The Beginning of Bop," 5, 52. I am indebted to Alan Kurtz for pointing me in the direction of these articles.
5. Kerouac, *The Dharma Bums*, 97–98.
6. Kerouac, *The Subterraneans*, 1.
7. These and the other headlines cited here come from a Google news search on the word *cool* conducted by the author on April 8, 2008.
8. Lazarus, "Gap Lost Its Basic Instinct," C-1.
9. Hirsch, *A Method to Their Madness*, 151.
10. Ibid., 205.
11. Howlett, *James Dean*, 61.
12. Truffaut, "Les Haricots du Mal," 40–41.
13. Howlett, *James Dean*, 72.
14. Bosworth, *Marlon Brando*, 20.

9 Live by the Swoosh, Die by the Swoosh

1. Huntley, *The World According to Y*, 152–153.
2. Pocock, *Can't Buy Me Love?*, 63.
3. Huntley, *The World According to Y*, 152, 156.
4. Zogby, *The Way We'll Be*, 123–124.
5. Majors and Billson, *Cool Pose*, xi.
6. Ibid., 54, 78.
7. Alexander, "Cool Like Me," 51–53.

10 America Loses Its Cool

1. Smith, "Remembering Teo Macero (1925–2008)."
2. McMillian, "Missing in Antiwar Action."
3. Denby, *Snark*, 1.
4. Goldfarb, "Democratic Wave in Congress," A29.
5. Deacon, "A New Year's Resolution."
6. Kessler et al., "The Prevalence and Correlates of DSM-IV," 669–678.

11 The Sound of Postcool Music

1. Ortega y Gasset, *The Dehumanization of Art*, 14.
2. Zogby, *The Way We'll Be*, 10–13.

12 The Postcool Society

1. Lasn, *Culture Jam*, 11.
2. Stearns, *American Cool*, 4.

Bibliography

Alexander, Donnell. "Cool Like Me: Are Black People Cooler Than White People?" *Utne Reader*, November–December 1997.

Anderegg, David. *Nerds: Who They Are and Why We Need More of Them*. New York: Tarcher/Penguin, 2007.

Ansermet, Ernst-Alexandre. "Bechet & Jazz Visit Europe, 1919." In *Frontiers of Jazz*. 2nd ed. Edited by Ralph de Toledano. New York: Frederick Ungar, 1962.

Armstrong, Elizabeth, ed. *Birth of the Cool: California Art, Design and Culture at Midcentury*. New York: Prestel, 2007.

Balliett, Whitney. *American Musicians*. New York: Oxford Univ. Press, 1986.

Berton, Ralph. *Remembering Bix*. New York: Harper & Row, 1974.

Bostrom, Meg. *The 21st Century Teen: Public Perception and Teen Reality*. Washington, DC: Frameworks Institute, 2001.

Bosworth, Patricia. *Marlon Brando*. New York: Viking, 2001.

Boulware, Marcus Hanna. *Jive and Slang of Students in Negro Colleges*. Hampton, VA: Hampton Institute, 1947.

Brady, Mildred Edie. "The New Cult of Sex and Anarchy." *Harper's*, April 1947.

Brinkley, Christina. "Inside a Salon That Serves the Logo-Phobic." *The Wall Street Journal*, November 15, 2007.

Broyard, Anatole. "A Portrait of a Hipster." *Partisan Review*, June 1948.

Büchmann-Møller, Frank. *You Just Fight for Your Life*. New York: Praeger, 1990.

Burley, Dan. *Dan Burley's Original Handbook of Harlem Jive*. New York, 1944.

Calloway, Cab. *Cat-ologue: A Hepsters Dictionary*. New York, 1938.

Carr, David. "Don't Aspire, Just Embrace Simplicity, Magazines Say." *The New York Times*, December 9, 2002.

Castiglione, Baldassare. *The Book of the Courtier*. Translated by Charles Singleton. New York: Anchor, 1959.

Condon, Eddie. *We Called It Music*. New York: Da Capo, 1992.

Cooper, Kenneth J., Hawkins Stern, and Arnold Mitchell. *Consumer Values and Demand*. Menlo Park, CA: Business Intelligence Program, SRI International, 1960.

Cottle, Michelle. "The Cool Presidency." *The New Republic*, March 4, 2009.

Cross, Gary. *The Cute and the Cool: Wondrous Innocence and Modern American Children's Culture*. New York: Oxford Univ. Press, 2004.

Davis, Miles, with Quincy Troupe. *Miles: The Autobiography*. New York: Touchstone, 1990.

Deacon, Michael. "A New Year's Resolution: Could We Be a Little More Polite, Please?" *The Telegraph* (London), January 1, 2009.

DeMichael, Don. "A Long Look at Stan Getz." *Downbeat*, May 19, 1966.

Denby, David. *Snark: It's Mean, It's Personal, and It's Ruining Our Conversation*. New York: Simon & Schuster, 2009.

Doherty, Daniel, and Amitai Etzioni, eds. *Voluntary Simplicity: Responding to Consumer Culture*. Lanham, MD: Rowman & Littlefield, 2003.

Elgin, Duane, and Arnold Mitchell. "Voluntary Simplicity." *CoEvolution Quarterly*, Summer 1977.

Francomano, Joe, Wayne Lavitt, and Darryl Lavitt. *Junior Achievement: A History*. Colorado Springs, CO: Junior Achievement, 1988.

Freeman, Bud, and Robert Wolf. *Crazeology: The Autobiography of a Chicago Jazzman*. Urbana: Univ. of Illinois Press, 1989.

Gaillard, Slim. *The Slim Gaillard Vout-o-Reenee Dictionary.*, n.d., ca. 1945.

Gates, Henry Louis. *The Signifying Monkey: A Theory of African-American Literary Criticism*. New York: Oxford Univ. Press, 1988.

Giddins, Gary, and Loren Schoenberg. "Jazz Dialogue: Gary Giddins in Conversation with Loren Schoenberg (Part One)." Jazz.com, May 20, 2008. www.jazz.com/features-and-interviews/2008/5/20/giddins-part-one.

Gioia, Ted. *West Coast Jazz*. Berkeley: Univ. of California Press, 1998.

Gladwell, Malcolm. "The Coolhunt." *The New Yorker*, March 17, 1997.

Gloor, Peter, and Scott Cooper. *Coolhunting: Chasing Down the Next Big Thing*. New York: AMACOM, 2007.

Goldfarb, Zachary A. "Democratic Wave in Congress Further Erodes Moderation in GOP." *The Washington Post*, December 7, 2006.

Gorlick, Adam. "'Integrity' Tops Web Dictionary's Lookups." *USA Today* (online), December 11, 2005. www.usatoday.com/tech/news/2005-12-11-integrity-word-of-year_x.htm.

Heath, Joseph, and Andrew Potter. *Nation of Rebels: Why Counterculture Became Consumer Culture*. New York: HarperCollins, 2004.

Hilbert, Robert. *Pee Wee Russell: The Life of a Jazzman*. New York: Oxford Univ. Press, 1993.

Hirsch, Foster. *A Method to Their Madness: The History of the Actors Studio*. New York: Da Capo, 2002.

Howe, Neil, and William Strauss. *Millennials Rising: The Next Great Generation*. New York: Vintage, 2000.

Howlett, John. *James Dean: A Biography*. London: Plexus, 2005.

Huntley, Rebecca. *The World According to Y: Inside the New Adult Generation*. Crows Nest, Australia: Allen & Unwin, 2006.

Keen, Judy. "Economic Survivalists Take Root." *USA Today*, April 14, 2009.

Kerouac, Jack. "The Beginning of Bop." *Escapade*, April 1959.

———. *The Dharma Bums*. New York: Penguin, 1976.

———. "The Last Word." *Escapade*, December 1960.

———. *The Subterraneans*. New York: Grove, 1958.

Kessler, Ronald C., Emil F. Coccaro, Maurizio Fava, Savina Jaeger, Robert Jin, and Ellen Walters. "The Prevalence and Correlates of DSM-IV Intermittent Explosive Disorder in the National Comorbidity Survey Replication." *Archives of General Psychiatry* 63 (2006): 669–678.

Klein, Naomi. *No Logo*. New York: Picador USA, 2000.

Koniarz, Bryan. "A Hipster's Dictionary." In accompanying booklet to *The Complete Lester Young Studio Sessions on Verve*, Polygram Records.

Lasn, Kalle. *Culture Jam: The Uncooling of America*. New York: Eagle Brook/Morrow, 1999.

Lazarus, David. "Gap Lost Its Basic Instinct." *San Francisco Chronicle*, January 26, 2007.

Leland, John. *Hip: The History*. New York: Harper Perennial, 2005.

Lewis, David, and Darren Bridger. *The Soul of the New Consumer: Authenticity—What We Buy and Why in the New Economy*. London: Nicholas Breely, 2000.

Lion, Jean Pierre. *Bix: The Definitive Biography of a Jazz Legend*. New York: Continuum, 2007.

MacAdams, Lewis. *Birth of the Cool: Beat, Bebop, and the American Avant-Garde*. New York: Free Press, 2001.

Majors, Richard, and Janet Mancini Billson. *Cool Pose: The Dilemmas of Black Manhood in America*. New York: Touchstone, 1993.

Manone, Wingy, and Paul Vandervoort. *Trumpet on the Wing*. New York: Doubleday, 1948.

McLuhan, Marshall. "The Southern Quality." *Sewanee Review* 55, no. 2 (July 1947): 357–383.

McMillian, John. "Missing in Antiwar Action." *The Washington Post*, January 20, 2007.

Mezzrow, Milton "Mezz," and Bernard Wolfe. *Really the Blues*. New York: Random House, 1946.

Mitchell, Arnold. *Lifeways and Life-Styles*. Menlo Park, CA: Business Intelligence Program, SRI International, 1973.

———. *The Nine American Lifestyles*. New York: Warner Books, 1984.

Noonan, Peggy. "Goodbye Bland Affluence." *The Wall Street Journal*, April 17, 2009.

Nugent, Benjamin. *American Nerd: The Story of My People*. New York: Simon & Schuster, 2008.

Nunberg, Geoffrey. "The Evolution of 'Lifestyle.'" *Fresh Air*, July 31, 2006. www.npr.org/templates/player/mediaPlayer. html?action=1&t=1&islist=false&id=5594617&m=5594618.

O'Neil, Paul. "The Only Rebellion Around: But the Shabby Beats Bungle the Job in Arguing, Sulking and Bad Poetry." *Life*, November 30, 1959.

Ortega y Gasset, José. *The Dehumanization of Art and Notes on the Novel*. Translated by Helene Weyl. Princeton, NJ: Princeton Univ. Press, 1948.

Penn, Mark J., with E. Kinney Zalesne. *Microtrends: The Small Forces Behind Tomorrow's Big Changes*. New York: Twelve/ Hachette Books, 2007.

Pocock, Barbara. *Can't Buy Me Love? Young Australians' Views on Parental Work, Time, Guilt and Their Own Consumption*. Manuka, Australia: The Australia Institute, 2004.

Pountain, Dick, and David Robins. *Cool Rules: Anatomy of an Attitude*. London: Reaktion Books, 2000.

Pressman, Gene. *Chasing Cool: Standing Out in Today's Cluttered Marketplace*. New York: Atria, 2007.

The Random House Dictionary of American Slang. Vol. 1 (A–G). Edited by J. E. Lighter. New York: Random House, 1994, 474–475.

Reich, Charles A. *The Greening of America*. New York: Bantam, 1971.

Robinson, James. "The Return of the Media Queen." *The Observer* (London), May 27, 2007.

Shin, Annys. "FTC Moves to Unmask Word-of-Mouth Marketing." *The Washington Post*, December 12, 2006.

Smith, Arnold Jay. "Remembering Teo Macero (1925–2008)." Jazz. com, February 24, 2008. www.jazz.com/jazz-blog/2008/2/24/ remembering-teo-macero-1925-2008.

Smith, Ethan, and Peter Lattman. "Download This: YouTube Phenom Has a Big Secret." *The Wall Street Journal*, September 6, 2007.

Southgate, Nick. "Coolhunting with Aristotle." *International Journal of Market Research* 45, no. 2 (Summer 2003): 167–189.

St. John, Warren. "Seriously, the Joke Is Dead." *The New York Times*, May 22, 2005.

Stanley, Thomas J., and William Danko. *The Millionaire Next Door*. Atlanta: Longstreet Press, 1996.

Stearns, Peter N. *American Cool: Constructing a Twentieth-Century Emotional Style*. New York: New York Univ. Press, 1994.

Sudhalter, Richard. *Lost Chords: White Musicians and Their Contribution to Jazz: 1915-1945*. New York: Oxford Univ. Press, 1999.

Sudhalter, Richard, Philip R. Evans, and William Dean-Myatt. *Bix: Man and Legend*. New Rochelle, NY: Arlington House, 1974.

Theado, Matt, ed. *The Beats: A Literary Reference*. New York: Carroll & Graf, 2003.

Thompson, Robert Farris. "An Aesthetic of Cool." *African Arts* 7, no. 1 (Autumn 1973).

Thorn, Jesse. "Finders Keepers." *The Sound of Young America*, May 21, 2005. http://tsoya.libsyn.com/index.php?post_id=7087.

Truffaut, François. "Les Haricots du Mal." *Cahiers du cinéma*, February 1956.

Turow, Scott. "When He Was Seventeen." *The New York Times Book Review*, March 9, 2008.

Upshaw, Lynn. *Truth: The New Rules for Marketing in a Skeptical World*. New York: AMACOM, 2007.

Windolf, Jim. "What's Funny Now?" *Rolling Stone*, September 18, 2008.

Zhong, Chen-Bo, and Geoffrey Leonardelli. "Cold and Lonely: Does Social Exclusion Literally Feel Cold?" *Psychological Science* 19 (2008).

Zogby, John. *The Way We'll Be: The Zogby Report on the Transformation of the American Dream.* New York: Random House, 2008.

... ...

... ...

Index

About the Author

Ted Gioia is a musician and author and has published six highly acclaimed books, including *Delta Blues*, *Work Songs*, and *West Coast Jazz*. Through his books and articles, he has established himself as one of the leading music writers and cultural critics of our times. Gioia's *The History of Jazz* was selected as one of the twenty best books of the year in *The Washington Post* and was a notable book of the year in *The New York Times*. He holds degrees from Stanford University, Oxford University, and Stanford's Graduate School of Business, and he previously served on the faculty at Stanford, where he helped establish the jazz studies program. In addition to recording several CDs as a jazz pianist, Gioia has also produced recording sessions by other artists. He is the president and editor of Jazz.com, a leading music-oriented website. Gioia has also been a consultant to Fortune 500 companies and has undertaken business projects in twenty-five countries on five continents. More information can be found at tedgioia.com.